Dance

Movements for body

SIMON AND SCHUSTER / NEW YORK

Blanche Howard

of the Self

mind and spirit

Published by Simon and Schuster
Rockefeller Center, 630 Fifth Avenue
New York, New York 10020
Designed by Edith Fowler
Manufactured in the United States of America
1 2 3 4 5 6 7 8 9 10

Library of Congress Cataloging in Publication Data:

Howard, Blanche Phillips.
  The dance of the self.

  1. Modern dance.   I. Title.
GV1783.H66   793.3'2   74-17232
ISBN 0-671-21838-7

I wish to thank my editor, Julie Houston, for her understanding and help in preparing *Dance of the Self* for publication. I would also like to thank Bern Porter for realizing its potentialities and for his valuable help. I am grateful to my husband, John Langly Howard, without whose encouragement and support this book would not have been written.

For my granddaughter, Becca,
with love

Contents

That dancing should be a way of reaching God is an idea foreign to our Western minds, yet it lies at the center of Hindu thought. The God, Shiva, created the world by dancing its first rhythm into being, and mortal man can attune himself to this cosmic motion, the source of the whole life process, through participation in its ritual. Dancers have always been attached to the temple, so that they might be used as an integral part of worship. Through the rhythmic movement of the dance, the individual attains poise and dignity in the flux of life, his soul is purified and he approaches that unity of being which is the goal of all human experience.

From the program notes for "The Dances of South India," a recital by Shanta Rao, one of the greatest classical dancers of India, presented on May 12, 1955, by the Juilliard School of Music in cooperation with the Museum of Modern Art in New York.

Foreword

I have notes on a method of teaching the dance which were sent to me about thirty years ago by a gifted and inspired teacher, Ellen Kearns. Those of us who had the good fortune to study with her have been immensely enriched, for she gave unstintingly, preparing the ground, planting the seeds, nourishing the plants and causing many lives to flower.

It was in the mid-1930s when I began to study dance with Ellen Kearns. At that time, I was a somewhat typical young New York woman who would have been repelled by any talk of spirituality, but I was enthralled by the extraordinary creative movements which resulted from simply letting go and allowing *it* to happen. *It* was the state of ecstasy of the dance that Ellen awakened in her students, unpremeditated and uncalculated, flowing through one's body. She taught how to awaken within oneself that force from which flow endless forms of dance, a force which can be likened to a fountain fed by a subterranean stream whose inexhaustible energy wells up into myriad expressions. Ellen was a deeply spiritual woman who was too wise to lecture while teaching. She loved the dance, and she loved teaching rhythm. She was convinced that man is inherently spirit, and she gave us all the extraordinary experience of the body being moved by spirit.

Among the notes on teaching that Ellen sent me were some that she had taken while studying and some that her teacher had taken during his studies. The emergence of the method of dance Ellen conveyed to her students can be likened to the children's circle game in which one player whispers a sentence to his neighbor, who in turn whispers it to his neighbor. The sentence makes the round of the circle until it comes back to the first player. By that time, it has changed from the original, sometimes even substantially in meaning. Such deviations had occurred as each succeeding teacher absorbed the methods of dance that were to be the cornerstones of Ellen Kearns's philosophy, a system of movement that from the beginning had had a deep spiritual quality and attracted spiritually minded people.

Generations moved on and pupils became teachers, and their pupils became teachers. Along the way, the concept of "rhythm" originated, coupled with the force of a strong Eastern philosophy. Ellen understood the productive variation that can take place in the teaching of dance. She wrote: "Each teaches from his own understanding, added to material received and applied, or absorbed and acted upon. This is then transcended by further study and practical application over a long period of time." To the system of dance that she inherited, Ellen added her own creative spirit and an ability to foster the creativity of others.

Ellen Kearns passed on a number of years ago, leaving behind the philosophy of rhythm and an extraordinary method of dance. "The teaching that I do," she wrote, "is only to uncover the deepest-down thing already in existence, man's perfection and wholeness. . . . That which is—call it Spirit, Divinity, Wholeness, Breath, God, the Absolute—comes into the nothingness of the body when the body lets go, when the mind lets go of the body, when emotions and desires let go of the mind, and both mind and body are in a renounced, annihilated, relaxed state. Deity comes through an open channel. . . . You can't do Rhythm. You live it. You are that thing. Your whole being reflects it, is absorbed by it."

Ellen's notes are a precious inheritance for all who seek to know themselves. That they may not be lost to posterity, I have sifted through them to write this book, in hopes that some of what she has given to me will come through to others. As a working artist, I have been deeply affected by her statement, "Line, Form—always think consciously of design in space and you will eventually function subconsciously." I have danced for more than thirty years, for the joy of it, and I believe that Ellen's notes will benefit others interested in studying or teaching dance, especially those far from centers of culture. This book will be a reminder that it is the spirit within us that dances. May it help you to alleviate the tensions that beset us all, and to develop your natural rhythmic flow so that you may discover the harmonies of your own being and the wellspring of creativity.

1
Rhythm and the Body

In man's physical body reside all the glories attainable in his long, unending pilgrimage of evolution. In it are stored all the possibilities of the spirit. All powers, all quantities, all characteristics ever intended for man's attainment are in the physical. But they must be glorified, spiritualized, deified. By way of the glorification and the spiritualization of the flesh, man may achieve oneness with the divinity within himself, and so with the divine life of the world. The body reflects the spirit. The body must be the spirit's channel of release, not its prison.

It might seem that rhythm just happens, without effort. This is not so. The body must be strengthened. The will must be used. There are definite techniques for arousing the flow of rhythm, and definite lessons are given in this book. You might liken the process to printing a photograph: in order to have a positive (wholeness, divinity, harmony), you must have a negative. In rhythm this means the body must be relaxed, renounced, abandoned.

The mind must be trained to relax, renounce and abandon itself to the pattern. Only then will the unscheduled, unplanned, uncalculated come into being and use the body to express its own fullness, peace, poise, joy. It will use the right or left arm or leg not as if right or left. It will use either or both as members of the same body.

The mind and will hold the body to the pattern of movement. Feeling and the imagination hold to the symbol and its quality. In this repetition, and lack of responsibility for the *kind* of movement that results, creativity is aroused and flows. This makes it possible for variations to happen, for the rhythm to catch hold and use the body as its instrument of expression. The mind rests from artful planning as the body is quickened and stirred to movement.

When the rhythmic pattern has been established for some time, the very walls of the instrument seem to fall away and the space inside joins the space in the room. Then the room space joins the outside space, which joins the sky.

The Orientals exemplify this with the space contained in an empty jar. The jar seems to contain only so much space, but the space inside and outside are the same. It is the all-pervading space (breath) which does not know that a certain portion of it has been enclosed and called by the name of a certain individual.

The specific movements that arouse the flow of rhythm are not greatly concerned with exercises as such, but with the process of freeing the body from tensions and constrictions so that rhythm can flow unimpeded. During this process, the body becomes strengthened, agile and fluid. The breathing becomes coordinated. One uses the breath with the movement. One moves on the breath, to the rhythm of one's own heartbeat and pulsing blood. It is a rhythm which is completely individual, yet at the same time, universal. This is the dance of Shiva, wherein endless forms are born, fall into nothingness, and are born again, on the same pattern but always different, like a symphony on a theme.

You establish the pattern. You move in the pattern and rest in it. The pattern is always maintained. While maintaining this pattern, you become aware of changes within it, of variations in timing, spacing, rhythmic pulsations, expansions, contractions, moods, feelings and levels of expression in mind, spirit and body. While you rest within the pattern, the movement continues, but slowly, even imperceptibly. The breathing slows down. As activity renews itself, the breath coordinates. Again and again, the energy leaks away into quietness, then spontaneously bursts into dance. This is not so-called expressionistic dancing, nor is it premeditated. It flows from the depths of the subconscious and from the heights of the supraconscious. The body becomes the instrument of a force that can move it through the whole gamut of expression. This includes animal rhythms and movements so angelic, so elevated and sustained that one is held suspended on the breath or feels the breath moving the body. The sense of weight is gone. One is all lightness, all air, all breath; or one can become so heavy, so immured in time, that the movement of an arm or a leg may take eons.

This dance, being a private or communal ecstasy, is not widely known. Its devotees have seldom used it for concert purposes, for the act of exhibiting takes away from its interiority.

The body as a whole must be kept properly tuned and in the peak of condition to be capable of complete expression in life and in the dance. It is important to know how to do this. Let us start with the diaphragm, which forms the base of the chest and the roof of the abdomen. The activity of the diaphragm, its flexions and tensions, affects one's heartbeat, breathing and circulatory system. Unconsciously, most people breathe in only to the top of the lungs, which is at best partial breathing. When the diaphragm is pulled down and the ribs and chest are expanded completely to all sides, the breath is drawn into all parts of the lungs.

The muscles of the diaphragm, back and abdomen should form a strong support for the torso. The torso should be well lifted from the thighs and legs. The space between the hips and the lower ribs, being the softest part of the body, can achieve the greatest stretch. It is this strong, stretched portion which gives the dancer long, beautiful lines. When this space becomes saggy or slack, the upper part of the body tends to sag toward the hips. This makes for "middle-age spread" and puts an undue strain on the hip muscles. Floor work strengthens the abdomen. When the abdominal muscles are slack, the vital abdominal organs will sag toward the pelvis and can become weakened. They should be held in place by inner muscular support. Stretching helps tone the inner muscles, and the movement of rhythm advances this conditioning process.

In rhythm, we think of the body as being composed of

CENTERS OF MOVEMENT
CENTERS OF FORCE
LINES OF ENERGY

The unchanging center of movement in rhythm is at the breastbone. Think of this place as an actual physical space through your body from front to back. Use your imagination. Feel it. Visualize it. We will call this the Center. Think of the head, arms and legs as radiating out from there. Think of the legs as being very long and dangling.

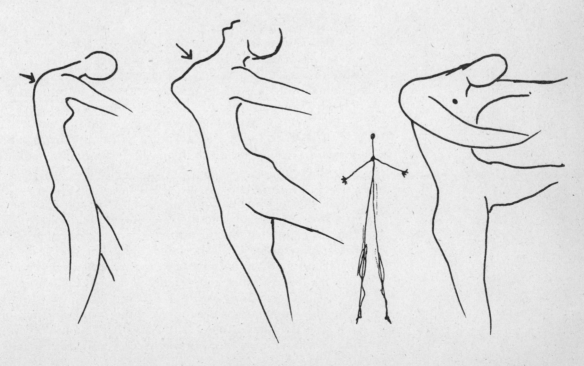

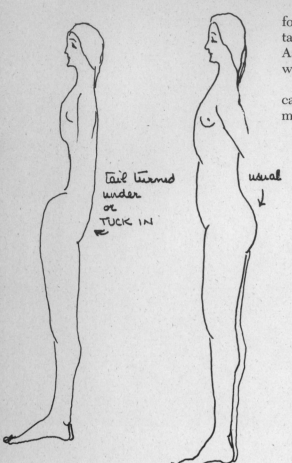

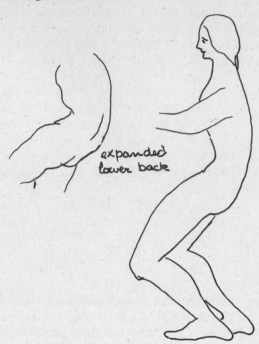

The very last few vertebrae at the end of the spine are a center of force and energy when curled in and under. Imagine that you have a tail which pulls down, in, under and up forward, curling in and around. Assume the position. In the directions for movement, this position will be indicated by the phrases "turn the tail under" or "tuck in."

By turning the tail under and pressing into the lower back, you can expand the space between the hips and the buttocks. This also makes for plasticity when moving backward.

Always turn the tail under when expanding the lower back, moving it or resting into it. The practice of expanding the lower back helps to prevent back trouble. When beginning a series of movements, be sure to start with a stretch, which will create the necessary spaces in the body and allow the tail to be tucked in and under more completely. We want to build an elastic tension, but not tenseness. It is helpful to think of the body as an upright column suspended in space.

To get a sense of the tucked-in tail, stand, turn your hands palms-forward, and make fists of them. At the same time, make a fist forward with the end of the spine. Another method is to visualize a fishhook and try to pull-push your tail forward into that position. Or, you can lie on the floor with your knees up, feet on the floor, and press your waist and lower back down to the floor. Imagine a diaper under you. Pull the lower end of the imaginary triangle up between the legs and toward the waist. With your mind, draw the other two ends around the waist and tie them with the lower point into a firm knot. You will find that the lower part of your torso will feel sturdy, strong and firm. The body soon becomes capable of holding the tucked-in position whenever desired, whether standing, leaping, sitting, crouching or lying.

The diaphragm, the Center and the expanded lower back (with the pelvic region and the turned-under tail) are the major movement

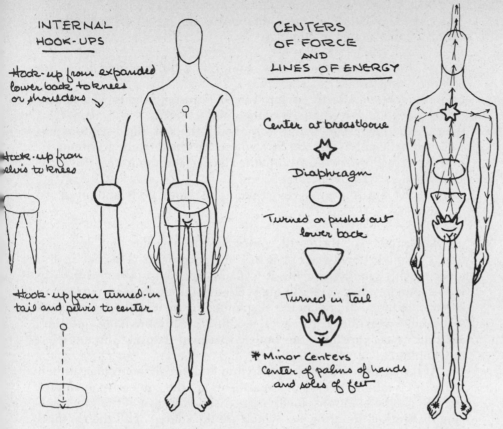

INTERNAL
HOOK-UPS

Hook-up from expanded
lower back to knees
or shoulders ↓

Hook-up from
pelvis to knees

Hook-up from turned-in
tail and pelvis to center

CENTERS
OF FORCE
AND
LINES OF ENERGY

Center at breastbone

Diaphragm

Turned or pushed out
lower back

Turned in tail

* Minor Centers
Center of palms of hands
and soles of feet

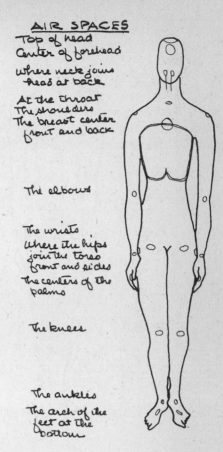

AIR SPACES
Top of head
Center of forehead
Where neck joins
head at back
At the throat
The shoulders
The breast center
front and back

The elbows

The wrists
Where the hips
join the torso
front and sides
The centers of the
palms

The knees

The ankles
The arch of the
feet at the
bottom

and force centers used in rhythm. One can visualize other lines of energy starting at any one of the centers and moving in any direction. A line of energy can begin at the tail, shoot up through the body, out the head and over in a high arc, much like a fountain.

Another useful visualization of the body is to imagine it as a series of seven units and six spaces, alternating.

UNIT 1: the head
SPACE 1A: the neck
UNIT 2: from the base of the neck to the breastbone
SPACE 2A: Center
UNIT 3: from the breastbone to the waist
SPACE 3A: the waist
UNIT 4: from the waist to the hip joints
SPACE 4A: hip joints
UNIT 5: from the hip joints to the knees
SPACE 5A: the knees
UNIT 6: from the knees to the ankles
SPACE 6A: the ankles
UNIT 7: the feet

The body functions as a whole. When any one part is used, the whole is affected, even though imperceptibly. If we energize any one center or move from it, the entire body reacts. Visualize the body as a single functioning organism, in which lines of force, air currents, the elements and connecting internal hook-ups all play their parts.

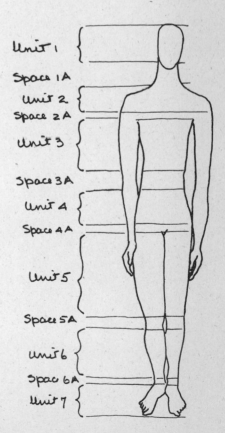

Unit 1
Space 1A
Unit 2
Space 2A
Unit 3
Space 3A
Unit 4
Space 4A
Unit 5
Space 5A
Unit 6
Space 6A
Unit 7

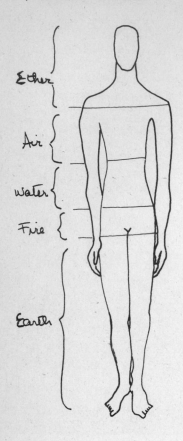

Ether

Air

Water

Fire

Earth

An ancient belief held that the body is composed of the elements earth, fire, water, air and ether.

EARTH: the basis or foundation, comprising the feet and legs; the bony structure.
FIRE: the force of energy, situated in the loins and the tucked-in end of the spine; the creativity of the mind.
WATER: the blood and fluids of the body; the soft, fluid sections between the pelvis and the ribs, where the vital organs are situated.
AIR: the actual breath drawn into the ribcage and the lungs; the air in which we live and breathe.
ETHER: the spirit, our innermost being, to which body and mind are subject.

The vitality of the earth comes up through the feet, legs and thighs through downward pressure on the ground. The pelvic fire feeds on this vitality, causing it to flame up. The updraft of the fire makes a high-rising, aerated lung section and then moves on to a high balance, to the feeling of being suspended in the air. The body seems to become weightless, part of the infinite. This breaking, melting, aerating process restores the body to its own natural, untrammeled functioning.

At the heart of the study of rhythm is the realization that, underlying all vibrations, cycles and heartbeats are the subjective analogies of feeling—the emotions, love, harmony and a sense of the great pulsing rhythms of the universe, which are the source of all the rhythms of life and nature. Rhythm deals directly with the autonomic nervous system, which regulates the cycles of movement and rest, activity and quiescence. The flow of rhythm is the flow of nature, where there is activity in rest, activity in activity, rest in rest and rest in activity.

The flow and rhythm of the seasons serves to enlarge awareness of the rhythmic flow within us. In the winter, when all growing things rest, concentration focuses on deep, underground movements. Spring suggests light, dancing, upward and growing, expanding and stretching. In summer, the natural movement is slow, soft, flowing, languorous stretches, large, broad, spreading. Autumn brings harvest and rejoicing—running, leaping, Bacchante-like movements.

2
The Breath and
Breathing Exercises

When you become conscious of your breathing, you notice that its rhythm is affected by what you think and feel. Notice how you breathe when you become excited and how you breathe when you feel calm and happy.

Become aware of the breath by breathing very slowly and gently. Feel as if you love your breath. Think of the quality of the air. Inhale as if you were breathing in the essence of nectar. Then breathe out as if a beloved friend were departing. When you consciously use the breath, you temporarily lose all sense of hurry, competition, ambition, getting somewhere. These have no part in rhythm, which is the fullness of the eternal now. If you want to sustain a sense of peace and fullness, try to breathe with full awareness of what you are doing. You are partaking of the natural world.

You can prevent physical exhaustion, too, by using your breath consciously, adjusting your movements and actions to the flow of the breath. In most of the movements given in this book, correlation with the breath is stressed.

In the study of rhythm you can think of five main breaths. Thinking or feeling the breath that *rises* will lift you onto your toes with chest high. Think of the breath that *descends*, and the chest is forced down with the knees tending to give. The breath that is *horizontal* will lead the body in full, round movements. The breath that *circulates* is the breath that you can think of as being anywhere in the body. The *general* breath is what we know as simple, unconscious inhaling and exhaling. You think you are doing the breathing. In reality, this breath functions for you: It is the life force, or *prana,* that moves your lungs. Each one of these five breaths has its funtion in the preservation and renewal of the body. They cooperate as one breath, without relapse, and without interference.

Breathing Exercises for Beginners

The exercises that follow concentrate on the main *down* breaths, which act as bellows, squeezing out the air that is already in the lungs. The action of these breaths is to give a blow to the solar plexus, which will force it to contract. A release with a sense of uplift follows.

ONE: SEA MURMUR. Stand tall with feet together. Blow the air forcefully out of the lungs through the mouth, treating your lungs as if you were wringing out a sponge. When the air is completely expelled, the lungs will refill automatically. It is important to continue blowing out until the lungs are completely empty. Tuck in and think of the lower back expanding. When the expansion is great enough, you will find yourself falling back into it. Fall back and back. Rest with your weight on the back foot. The "up-through" line—the release from the tucked-in tail and the in-rush of breath—can lead you into spirals and then onto your toes.

TWO: EARTH BREATHING. This is basically the same action as above, but done on the floor with the legs spread wide. The expulsion of air sends energy out the nerve ends of the fingertips and toes, and the pressure pushes the navel and Center down. Repeat.

THREE: Breathe out forcefully in one of three ways—as if you were blowing at a floating feather, or against a frosted windowpane, or at the flame of a candle. Which symbol you choose will depend on the effect you want to achieve, or what you want to lead into. If you visualize a floating feather, your body will follow the mouth action up, lifting the head from the breastbone Center. If you want the movement to be straight forward on the horizontal plane, visualize the frosted windowpane or lighted candle. The head will eventually arc upward and back, ridding one of tension and congestion. The rhythmic impulse will flow unimpeded as the nerves of the vertebrae are freed of all weight.

The greater and more forceful the blowing, the greater the extent of the over-arc, i.e. the body stretching up and back, until the whole torso is moved backward from the base of the spine. Knees and ankles fold and reflex, or rebound up. The movement becomes serpentine or like a whip snapping. This exercise breaks up resistance, heaviness, solidity, opacity, and makes the mind and body more pliable. It should be done when the body is warm, after rest from a workout.

FOUR: Breathe in through the nostrils slowly, as if you were smelling a flower. Hold your breath. Think of the eyes, ears and the top of the head as expanding. The weight of the head will lift from the top of the spine and out of the center. Exhale through the nostrils very slowly. You can do the same exercise forcefully and quickly at first to release tightness and tension, and then proceed to a slower version, which is excellent as a preliminary to walking and being upheld on the breath.

FIVE: Stand with one foot in front of the other, your weight on the front foot. Breathe in strongly through the nostrils. This should gradually bring you up onto your toes. Bring the back leg forward as if it were dangling from the high breastbone Center. As you become more advanced, you will begin to stretch the back leg as it moves forward. When the back foot is in front, transfer your weight to it as you exhale. This nostril breathing clears the spaces in the head.

SIX: Breathe in through the nostrils and out through the mouth. This pulls the abdominal muscles in and releases the diaphragm, and can eventually force the tail in and under. When this happens, you can feel a tightening and an inner line of energy coming up through.

SEVEN: Breathe in through the nostrils until the chest wall expands to its fullest capacity. Hold that expansion while breathing out and think of a straight line coming down through the body and contracting the abdominal muscles. Breathe in a second time, trying to expand the lower ribs even more. Breathe out slowly and completely. Repeat. Do this exercise slowly and firmly.

EIGHT: FOREST BREATHING. Feet apart, tuck in, knees bent, arms hang at sides. Think down through the feet into imaginary taproots under the earth. Press down and as the legs straighten a line of energy comes up through. The arms lift from the sides, to shoulder level. The head is held high. Breathe in deeply, feeling as if you are one of many trees in a forest, as if you are breathing in the air of the forest. The arms move down and the knees give as you breathe out. Breathe in and out deeply and slowly, with great concentration.

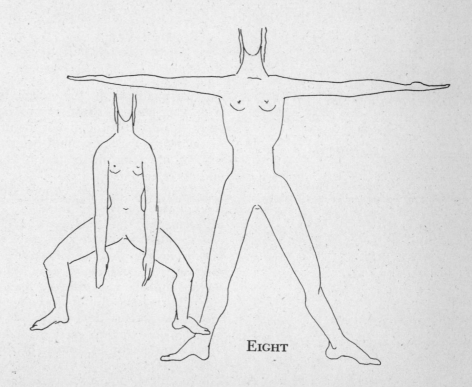

EIGHT

3
Symbols and Rhythm

The quality of the symbol and the feeling it engenders are its life force. Consciousness responds to that life force subjectively, then the body expresses it through movement. Anything that captures the imagination will do as the symbol, but nature is the prime source, with the seasons, elements, minerals, and vegetable and animal life providing endless related images.

Think of water in its various aspects—the ocean, a lake, a pond, a river, a brook: mist, fog, rain, snow. Each evokes a different mood, a different quality of feeling. Thoughts of snow or rain or any other water symbol will each affect the nervous system in a different manner. When you think of snow, you may think of something soft and melting, or of cold winter, or of being swirled by the wind. Snow can be thought of as a covering for the earth, under which growing things sleep. It can be restful. It can be weightless. Concentrating on weightlessness will cause the body to feel light. When you think of rain, you may think of a tingling excitement or of a warm gentleness.

Do not skimp in the use of your imagination as a motive force. Learn to rely on it. There will be many symbols given in the lessons, but the creative mind will search for original ones. Think creatively of all the many aspects of fire—glowing embers, licking flames, fires that seethe and sizzle; hearth fires, forest fires, cooking fires, bonfires and volcanoes. Concentrate hard on any one of these and you will generate a movement akin to it.

Think of work symbols, such as planting, sowing, reaping, or even rowing. And don't ignore mechanical objects or toys—they can also be useful. The symbol quiets the mind, which rests in it. Concentrate on the symbol and you will come to the feeling. The body responds automatically to feeling, but if you use the will, you may use the wrong muscles. Do not try to direct movement. It happens as a result of concentration.

First create the pattern of the movement. When this is established, work more specifically with the symbol itself. For example, if the symbol were a rolling hoop, you would not think of yourself as a rolling hoop. Get a mental image of a rolling hoop. Think of its qualities, roundness, rolling. You want the free moving image, not the object. Keep returning to the qualities. Another example would be the bear symbol. If you played the bear, that would be a simile, not a symbol. Use your imagination. How does he move? He has soft strength. He is shaggy. What quality impresses you?

Concentrate on a forest breathing. Think of one tree until you think-feel *tree* and the body, which at first is heavy and in the way, finally becomes eliminated. Then allow your mind to expand to encompass the forest and, in the release of concentrating on hundreds of trees breathing, come back to the one, the tree of life; but you never come back to thinking of yourself as moving or breathing. The movement happens. Keep the symbol in your mind. Keep the body to the pattern. The rhythm will happen. This is the release, the upwelling of the spirit. Trying to hurry or force the release will cause tension. Feel as if you have all the time in the world. Know and trust the creativity within you, then it can be released. It is like the fragrance of a flower. It is there.

4
Rhythm as Expressed in Body Movement

We are part of nature's rhythm, the rhythm that moves the tides, changes the seasons, causes seeds to grow to maturity and then to develop seeds again. In the study of rhythm, we open ourselves to the beneficence of nature. Our own nature unfolds, and the flow of creativity within ourselves begins. We become aware of how energy can build up, fall away and then renew itself. We learn through our experience that by letting go of the old we can create mental and physical space for the new to come through.

The process of creative movement comes from the formal pattern and from the idea, or symbol. The mind rests while movement, form and variations flow as if from a never-ending stream. One does not move, but is moved.

The spirit moving through the body can at first throw it into chaotic motion. As we work on the exercises and develop technique, the spirit will move the body into freedom, *but in form*. You must not try to force yourself into form because that would be allowing your finite mind to take over. The creative spirit will, in its own time, make its own forms.

Do not be upset if you come to a period when you feel all weight and heaviness, as if your feet were rooted—when it takes forever for one movement to happen, as if indeed you were moving very heavy weights. Know that this is but a stage. Go with your whole self into any rhythmic stage that comes. Feel timeless. If nothing happens, be part of the nothing. The demanding mind must be removed from the whole process of rhythm.

The following exercises will help to make the body a fitting instrument through which rhythm can flow. Just as a musician must develop his technique so that the spirit of music can be expressed, one who dances needs such discipline as will enable the body to accept the demands of a creative and fluid spirit.

Stretches

Always begin every exercise or lesson with a stretch. In this way, you can develop long lines, lift the chest wall, make space at the waist, make room for a complete tuck-in. The lower and upper back stretches make for freedom of movement. Stretches develop spaces between the vertebrae and help in the prevention of back trouble.

ONE: Yawn, pull up and stretch all over.

TWO: This is the Jacob's Ladder stretch, which will begin many of our lessons. Feet together, stretch up through fingertips, first on one side, then on the other. Keep heels down. Try to feel as if you are climbing a ladder, reaching higher each time you stretch up.

TWO

THREE: OFFERING OF PICKED FRUITS SYMBOL. One arm comes up as if to pick fruit from a tree, then the other comes up. They both pull up and come over together in an arc to one side at waist level. Repeat to the other side. Repeat.

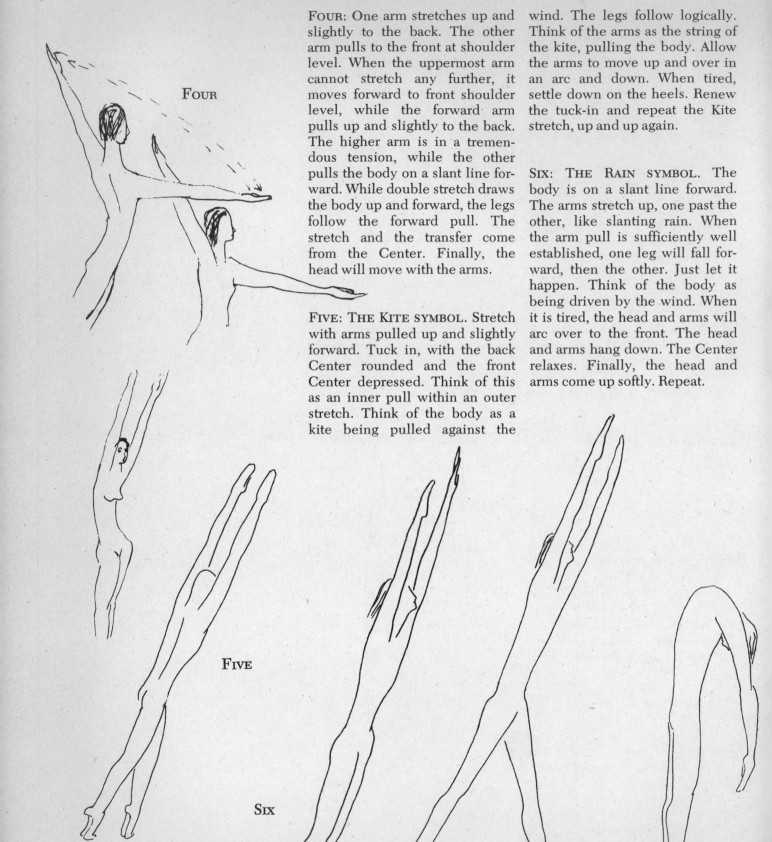

FOUR: One arm stretches up and slightly to the back. The other arm pulls to the front at shoulder level. When the uppermost arm cannot stretch any further, it moves forward to front shoulder level, while the forward arm pulls up and slightly to the back. The higher arm is in a tremendous tension, while the other pulls the body on a slant line forward. While double stretch draws the body up and forward, the legs follow the forward pull. The stretch and the transfer come from the Center. Finally, the head will move with the arms.

FIVE: THE KITE SYMBOL. Stretch with arms pulled up and slightly forward. Tuck in, with the back Center rounded and the front Center depressed. Think of this as an inner pull within an outer stretch. Think of the body as a kite being pulled against the wind. The legs follow logically. Think of the arms as the string of the kite, pulling the body. Allow the arms to move up and over in an arc and down. When tired, settle down on the heels. Renew the tuck-in and repeat the Kite stretch, up and up again.

SIX: THE RAIN SYMBOL. The body is on a slant line forward. The arms stretch up, one past the other, like slanting rain. When the arm pull is sufficiently well established, one leg will fall forward, then the other. Just let it happen. Think of the body as being driven by the wind. When it is tired, the head and arms will arc over to the front. The head and arms hang down. The Center relaxes. Finally, the head and arms come up softly. Repeat.

SEVEN: BENDING AND REACHING. Legs apart at a comfortable distance, keep the body as straight as possible, lifting the Center. Bend over forward straight from the hips, keeping the back straight. Stretch to the left, then to the right, as far as possible. Maintaining the stretch, come up facing right. Reach up, then pull down on the left side, to hip height and come to the Center. Reach forward and stretch up. Repeat, coming straight down, stretch to the right side, then to the left and pull up on the left side.

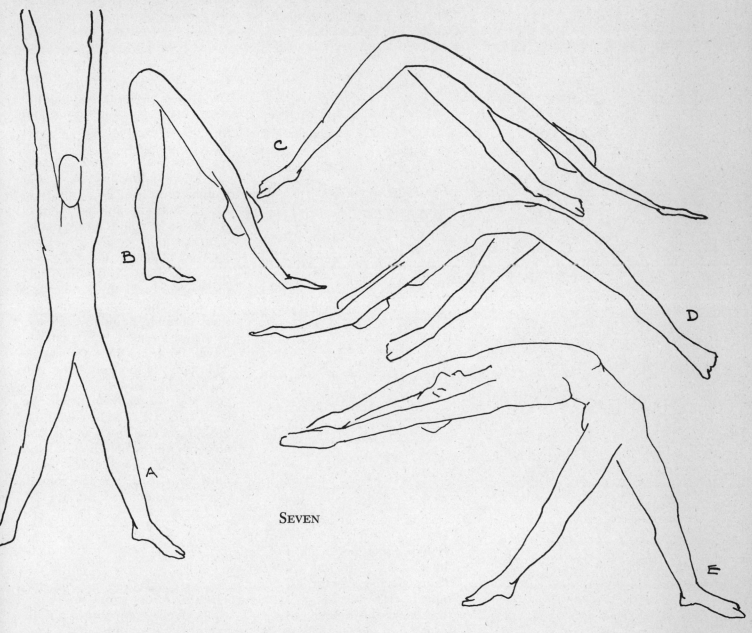

SEVEN

Movements to Release the Center

These exercises help to make the space through the breastbone, or the Center, pliable and alive.

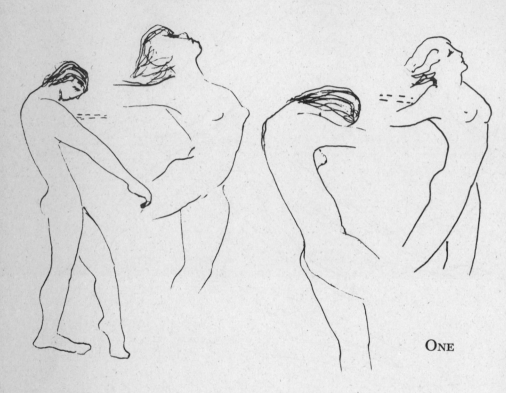

ONE

ONE: POLES PUSHING THE CENTER FORWARD AND BACKWARD SYMBOL. With one foot in front of the other, face straight ahead. Imagine a pole coming from behind and pushing the Center forward. Let your weight shift slightly to the front foot. Let the arms hang relaxed. Imagine the pole now coming from the front, pushing the Center back. Transfer the weight to the back foot. Again the pole pushes forward, to the furthest possible point, then to the furthest possible point to the back. You find yourself being pushed forward until, at the furthest possible point to the front, after falling straight forward—not down—you feel the movement to the back, and fall straight backward, not down. This leads into a free movement in which the head and arms are involved. The Center must become alive before the tail can become alive.

TWO: THE GOLDEN THREAD SYMBOL. One foot in front of the other, face straight forward. Think of the Center as being pulled forward by a golden thread. As the thread pulls, the Center and the feet follow. They must follow where the thread draws them. Eventually you will feel as if you are winged. All concentration is on the Center.

THREE: After strenuous work, when feeling breathless, walk, moving forward through the Center. The back leg will dangle forward, as the Center rises. The weight shifts to the front foot as the Center relaxes down. The Center can lift and then move forward, or just move forward. Use music with various rhythms. The Center will respond.

FOUR: THE PEACOCK WALK SYMBOL. Stand with one foot in front of the other. Think up through the head, very tall, abdominal wall contracted. Tuck the tail in. Bring the back knee forward and up fairly high. Then think out through the big toe and stretch the leg out to the front. Lower the leg so that the big toe touches the ground first. As the Center moves forward, the arms fold back and out in a movement from the Center to the shoulder joints and to the back. Finish with the arms stretched back at shoulder level. Their movement flows from the shoulder joints to the elbows, the elbows to the wrists, the wrists to the fingertips. The weight comes forward onto the front foot. The Center relaxes back in, and the arms come around to the front. The other leg is then drawn slowly and heavily up, knee first, and stretched out through the big toe. Repeat.

FIVE: THE CANDLE SYMBOL. Remember, it is important to fix your imagination firmly on the

FOUR

symbol. Think of the Center as the flame of a candle. Think of the shoulders and the weight of the body as wax, melting away. The flame burns up through the head, which feels lighter and lighter, while the outside circumference of the body feels heavier and heavier. Repeat.

Inner Stretches Up Through

ONE: The arms pull up and fall down and pull up and fall down. Keep repeating. Do it on a bounce, a double bounce, a triple bounce; then from side to side, and up over and around.

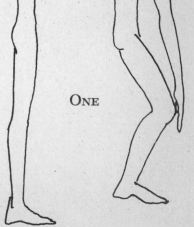

ONE

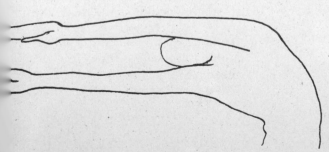

Then up over to one side, up around and over to the other side

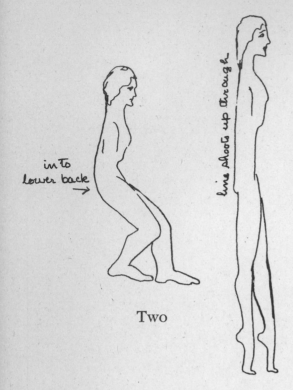

TWO

TWO: Assume a half-sitting position with knees bent, one foot in front of the other, and the end of the spine tucked in. Bounce down hard on heels. The energy should rebound up from the end of the spine and out through the head. This will straighten the knees and bring you up onto your toes. Then bounce down on your heels again, into a half-sit. Keep the lower back rounded in this position. You can move forward while up on your toes.

THREE: THE TURTLE SYMBOL. Stand with heels together and tail tucked in. Hold the head up high, pulling your chin in, and arch the back of your neck like a horse. Now stretch up at the back of your neck as you continue to force your chin in. Feel eye spaces where the head and neck join. Slap the spaces smartly. Then slowly draw your shoulders up as high as possible. Head and neck slip down in as low as possible. When the head cannot be lowered any further, let it come up slowly and the shoulders come down. Stretch the head up; push the shoulders down. After repeating several times, when the head is at the highest point, turn it to one side, then to the other. Repeat.

THREE

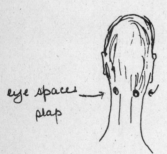

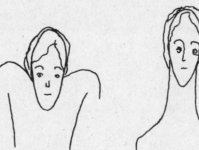

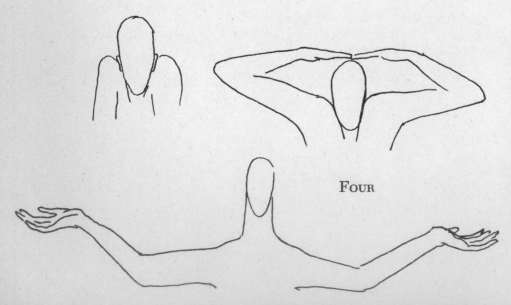

FOUR

FOUR: In the half-sitting position, tuck the tail in and draw the shoulders up as far as they will go toward your ears. Draw the elbows upward, then the wrists, then the hands and then the fingers, which meet on the top of the head. Let the head rest on the collarbone, with the chin in. Stretch the back of the neck long. Then very slowly let the head come up as you press the shoulders down. This will also release the elbows. Press the elbows down, and you will release the wrists. Press with the wrists and the hands will come up and out. Do all this as the head is coming up. Think up through the head. Repeat.

FIVE: Do the same, but raise the shoulders up and around toward the front. This should move the head forward from the Center. Release up. Repeat.

SIX: Shoulders to the back. The fingers meet at the back of the head. The head moves to the back from the Center. Release up. Repeat.

SEVEN: PILLOW LOSING ITS FEATHERS SYMBOL. This is an over-arc from side to side, from heaviness to lightness to heaviness. Think up through the head. Then arc it up and over to one side, where the head hangs heavily. Give it a slight shaking, as if shaking feathers from a pillow. The head then floats up and over to the other side. Repeat several times.

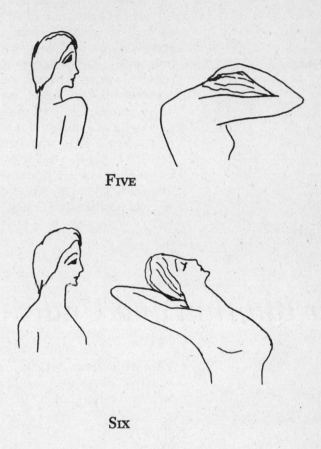

FIVE

SIX

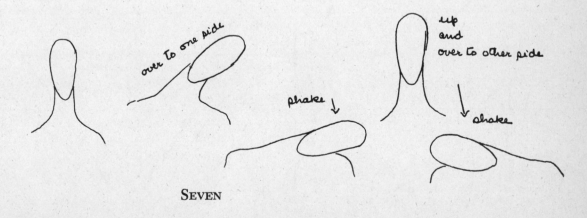

SEVEN

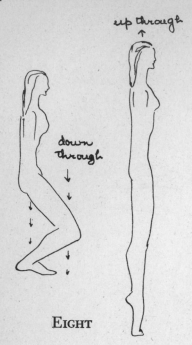

down through

up through

EIGHT

EIGHT: A LINE UP THROUGH—STRAIGHT AND NARROW. Concentrate on the straight line coming up through the head. Feet together, and a strong tuck-in. Keep the lower back rounded, stomach sucked in, knees bent, heels pressed down and the chest high (not out). The energy of the pelvis pushing upward and the pressure of the heels pushing down causes a line of energy to move up through and out the top of the head. Keep the heels together so that the two legs move together as one, as if you were a mermaid. Then come back to the original position and repeat.

NINE: Start in an upright position, one leg in front of the other. Think of air in the chest pressing upward into the top of the chest. Keep this sense of uprightness as you skip or walk or stand still.

After you have worked on the inner stretches up through for some time (perhaps months) your body will finally respond by feeling the phrasing and balancing of its own rhythms and of the music. The head moves in over-arcs up from the Center. The more you press down through the pelvis and feet, the greater the rebound to lightness and leaps. (For more about music, see pp. 54–55.)

Under Rhythm and Under-Arcs

Feet wide apart, tuck in and assume a half-sit position. Think of a deep rhythm moving under the earth from one of your feet to the other. Your weight moves onto one foot. Press down on that foot

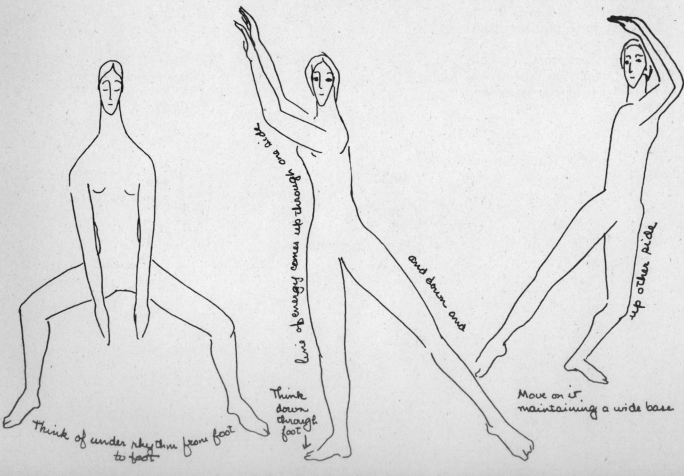

Think of under rhythm from foot to foot

line of energy comes up through one hip

Think down through foot

and down and

up other side

Move on it, maintaining a wide base

and the line of energy will straighten that leg and that side of the body, and feel as if it is coming out the top of the head, making a long line. Resume the half-sitting position and think down through the same foot, into the floor and under to the other foot.

The line will come up through on that side. When the rhythm is established, let the arms move with it. Both arms move to the side of the rising rhythm and follow the pattern, up one side, down, across and up the other. When the whole movement is suffi-ciently established, move on it. As the rhythm comes up on one side, the other leg is freed at the hip and moves forward, maintaining a wide angle. As you come down, bring the leg down and move across with bent knees to that side and up. Repeat.

The Feet and the Earth

ONE: SMITING AND STAMPING WITH FEET. Place one foot in front of the other, about a foot apart. Pull the arms down to the front with fists clenched. Keep a strong tuck-in. Press down on the front foot. Feel the line of energy coming up through as the arms pull down longer. Raise the knee of the back leg as it moves forward, pull into your lower back and smite the earth with your foot, emphasizing the heel, twice. At the same time, bend your elbows and bring your fists up to waist level. Press down on new front foot as the line of energy comes up through and the arms pull straight down. Repeat.

TWO: THE PANTHER SYMBOL. Heavy, soft moving. Start with the end of the spine well tucked in. Bend the knees slightly and put one foot in front of the other. Move as if you were a cat going downhill in soft slush. Feel each step carefully first with the heel, then with the center of the foot, then the ball of the foot. Then press down hard, putting your weight on the front foot. Move the back foot forward. Transfer of weight is accomplished through the pelvic grip. This should be a soft-footed, resilient movement, done with a soft, rounded back.

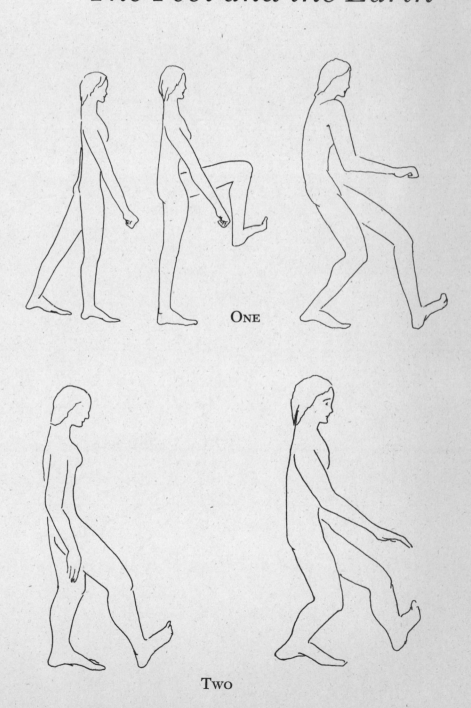

ONE

TWO

THREE

THREE: THE PRANCING HORSE SYMBOL. Transfer of weight. Fold the arms at the elbows and raise them to shoulder height. Lift one knee high to the chest and down. Lift the other knee and stamp down. Stand in one place for a while, then prance forward. Keep the head and chest high, and the lungs full of air.

FOUR: FEET SINKING INTO SOFT MOSS SYMBOL. With one foot in front of the other, bend the knees slightly. The front foot sinks down into the moss and makes a small rebound up into a small leap. Sink, step, step, then small leap. Then the other foot sinks into moss: repeat, step, step, small leap. The leap becomes larger, the rebound stronger. The leap becomes greater, wider and freer. Retain the pattern of sink, step, step, leap.

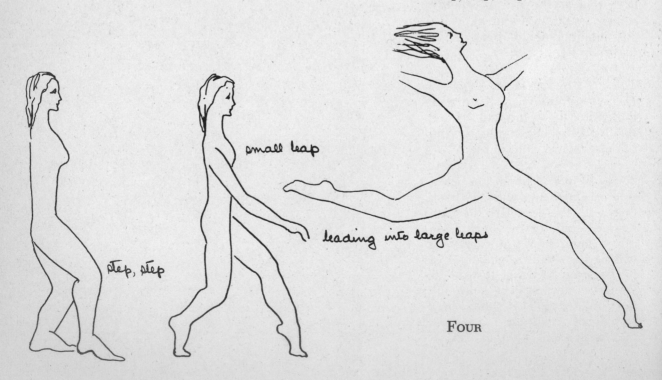

step, step

small leap

leading into large leaps

FOUR

Swinging and Swaying

ONE: THE SICKLE MOON SYMBOL. Stand with legs apart. Tuck in. Half-sit. Let both arms swing up to one side and straighten the legs at the same time. Bring the arms down to Center level and half sit again. Raise the arms to the other side and straighten the legs. When the coordinated patterns of the arms and legs are established, swing the arms up to one side, down and up to the other, back down and up the other side and over the head—around and down and up. Swing down and up, down and up, down and up over the head, and around, down and up. If the arms come up over the head from the left side, the next time they go over the head, it will be from the right. As the arms come over the head the feet come together, and they separate as the arms move down to the side. The knee bends on whichever side the arms are coming down, and straightens as the arms move up. A small jump can develop on the up-through. Then, as the arms swing up over the head, the small jump evolves into a half turn. Complete the turn as the arms move down. Repeat. This becomes a high, joyous movement. It is an exhilarating way to end a lesson.

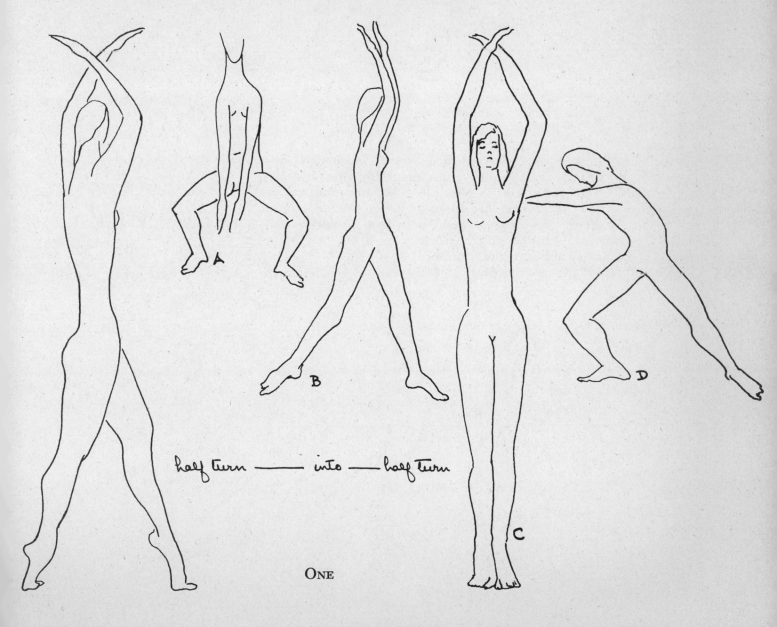

half turn —— into —— half turn

ONE

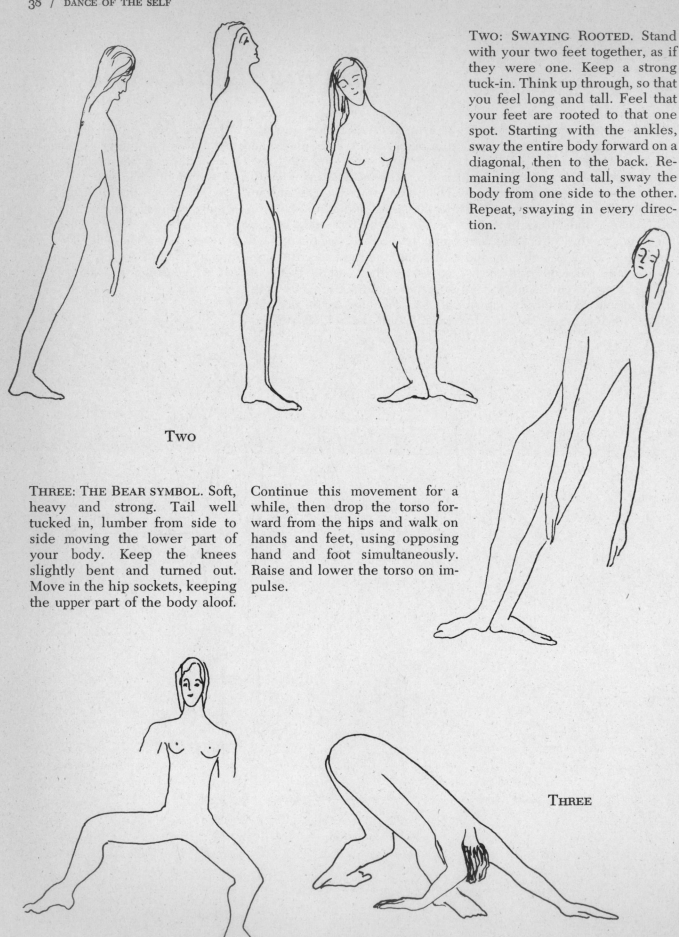

TWO: SWAYING ROOTED. Stand with your two feet together, as if they were one. Keep a strong tuck-in. Think up through, so that you feel long and tall. Feel that your feet are rooted to that one spot. Starting with the ankles, sway the entire body forward on a diagonal, then to the back. Remaining long and tall, sway the body from one side to the other. Repeat, swaying in every direction.

Two

THREE: THE BEAR SYMBOL. Soft, heavy and strong. Tail well tucked in, lumber from side to side moving the lower part of your body. Keep the knees slightly bent and turned out. Move in the hip sockets, keeping the upper part of the body aloof.

Continue this movement for a while, then drop the torso forward from the hips and walk on hands and feet, using opposing hand and foot simultaneously. Raise and lower the torso on impulse.

THREE

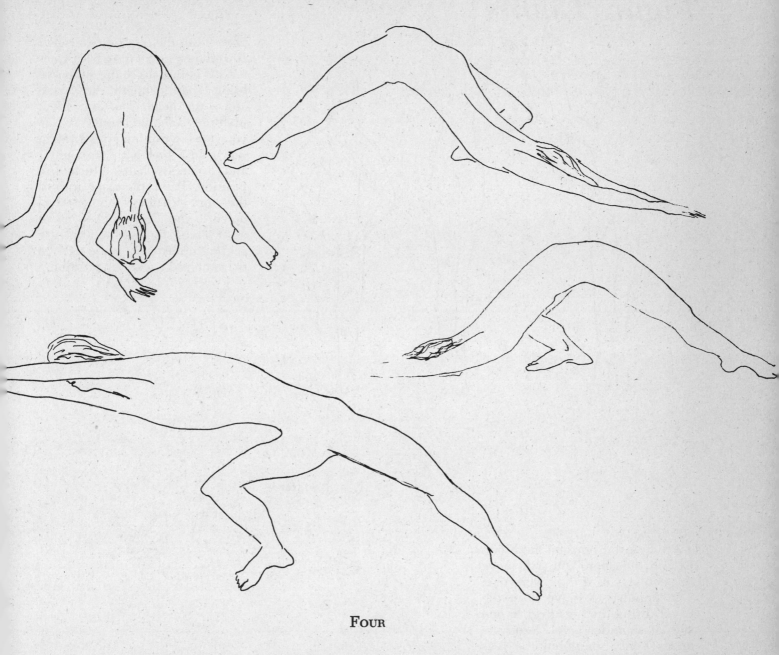

FOUR

FOUR: ELEPHANTS MOVING THROUGH THE FOREST. The elephants move heavily, mightily. Hang over forward from the end of the spine and begin to sway the body heavily from side to side. Continue for a while. Then let the leg on the side opposite the sway be lifted by the weight of the body and move forward. Swing back to that side, lift the other leg and move forward. Although the movement is heavy, it is also relaxed, and the torso loosens.

Figure Eights

ONE: With the feet together, half sit and tuck in. Starting from Center, lift both arms to one side and bring them straight up high above the head. The movement up through should bring you onto your toes. Drop the arms straight down on a line with the Center and resume the half-sit, tucked-in position. Raise the arms toward the other side, over the head and down to the Center. Then move on it, step, step, as the arms are coming up. Always come back to the centered, tucked-in position.

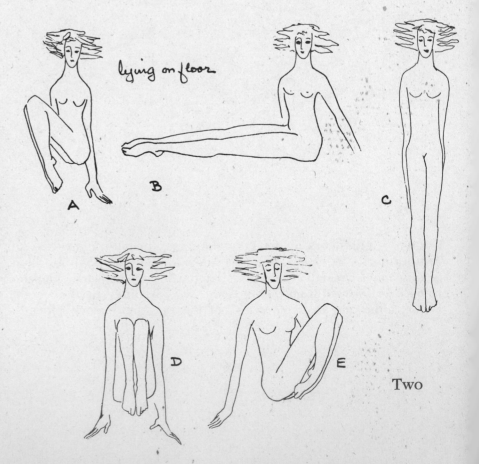

lying on floor

TWO: Figure Eights on the Floor. Lie on the floor. You will move the two legs as if they were one. The impulse to move is at the navel. Bring the legs over to one side at shoulder level. Keep the knees bent. Straighten the legs and move them slowly down, so that the body is in a straight line. Draw the knees up to the chest and allow them to fall over to the other side at shoulder level. Then straighten the legs and move them down to a straight line. Repeat, first to one side, then to the other. Start slowly, then move quickly, then move slowly again.

TWO

THREE: You can also do figure eights with shoulders, elbows and wrists. Work first on one side for some time, then the other, then both in continuous alternation. Press the shoulder down, push it forward, pull it up and around to the back and press down. Then push it back, raise it as high as it can go, bring it around forward and press down. Repeat the whole movement. The elbow, then the wrist do the same. The movement becomes continuous—shoulder, elbow, wrist and out the fingertips. Work for a while again on each part alone. Do the same with hips, into the knees and ankles.

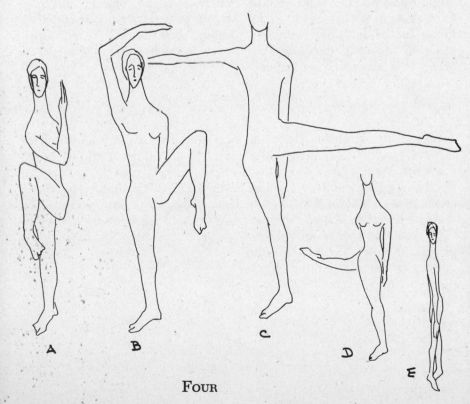

A   B   C   D   E

FOUR

FOUR: This exercise should be done after the one above. It is a kind of walk, opposing arm and leg. With one foot in front of the other, raise the knee of the front leg and the elbow of the opposite arm. Each moves across the body, so that they pass each other. Then both move higher and circle out, each to its own side, and extend to full length. They describe circles toward the back, then around to the front again and down, maintaining the extended position. Then the other arm and leg move to the front. Repeat, first one side, then the other.

Rotaries

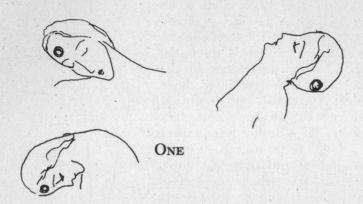

ONE

ONE: THE LITTLE SPHERE INSIDE OF THE BIG SPHERE. A head rotary. A weight (a little sphere) is inside the head (a big sphere). The head hangs from the base of the neck. It moves slowly with the feeling of having a small but heavy ball rolling inside. The head rotates slowly and smoothly, around and around. Think up through. Tuck in tightly. Head rotation slows down and stops.

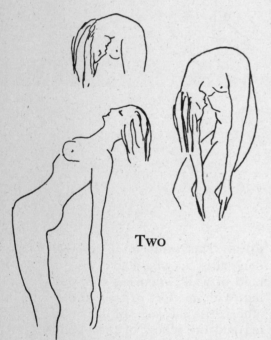

TWO

TWO: POPPIES UNDER A HOT SUN. Your head is as if it were a heavy poppy head. A gentle wind blows it around and up. It hangs first from the base of the head, then from the base of the neck. The wind blows the poppy head around and up. Let it go around for some time before it sinks lower in the hot sun, from one place to the next, one after the other. It is always blown up and then droops lower, rotating from the neck, to the throat, to the Center, to below the breast, to the waist, to the hips. Keep the head at hip level for a long time. Keep a strong tuck-in, pushing through to the front at the hips and crotch. Then relax the torso completely as you concentrate on circling the knees, then the ankles, and drop down to the floor.

THREE: SEEDS DROP OUT OF POPPY HEAD. The seeds go into the earth. You lie on your side, head and knees as close together as possible. Think of a blanket of leaves burying the seeds deeper in the earth. The body relaxes down and down. Think of the sun getting hotter and hotter every day and the seeds beginning to stir. Contract in at the Center, then relax. Repeat a few times. Think of seeds stretching out rootlets. Turn over onto your back, slowly and languorously. Stretch

THREE

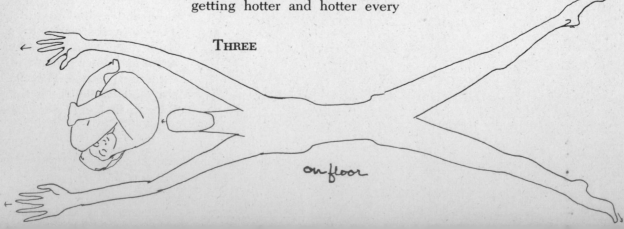

on floor

out from the Center through your head, arms and legs. Spread the legs wide apart. Then roll over to the other side and curl in. Uncurl and repeat the stretch. Cross one leg over the other in a long scissors stretch. The leg pulls and turns over, then the upper body. Continue the movement in that direction across the room, then to the other side across the room. Then as you roll to one side, contract with the head and knees together and roll over onto your knees. Bring one knee up so that the foot is on the floor. Move your torso around and spiral up. Stretch, collapse to the floor, and spiral up.

FOUR: HIP ROTARY. Feet together, swing the pelvic region back and forth a few times. Move your hips from side to side. Think of a pole pushing in at one hip socket; the other hip will move out. The pole pushes so hard that it makes you take small steps to the side. Keep feet close together. Then think of the pole pushing to the other side, so that that hip will push out. Do it from side to side for a while, then move hips in a circle in one direction, then in the other. Then walk with the hips moving in a circle.

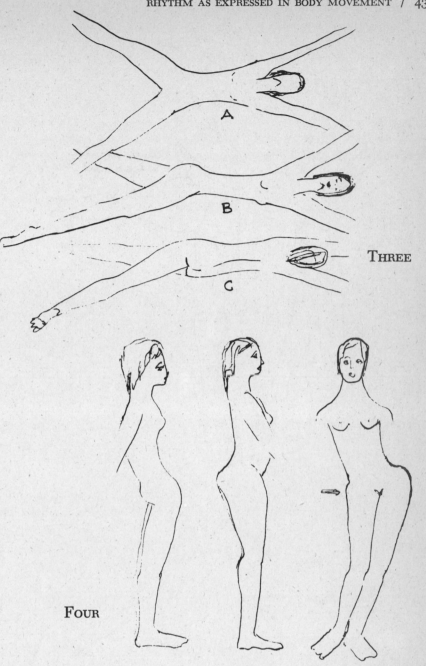

THREE

FOUR

ONE

Spirals and Twists

ONE: MIST AROUND THE MOUNTAIN. With arms front and rounded at shoulder level, move one arm slowly around to the back. Let the eyes follow the movement of the elbow. The other arm trails after in a round sweep. Hold the head high. Then bring both arms to the front and move the other arm to the back. The movement of the arms will pull the body around in a circle. Then legs follow. Continue with the following exercise.

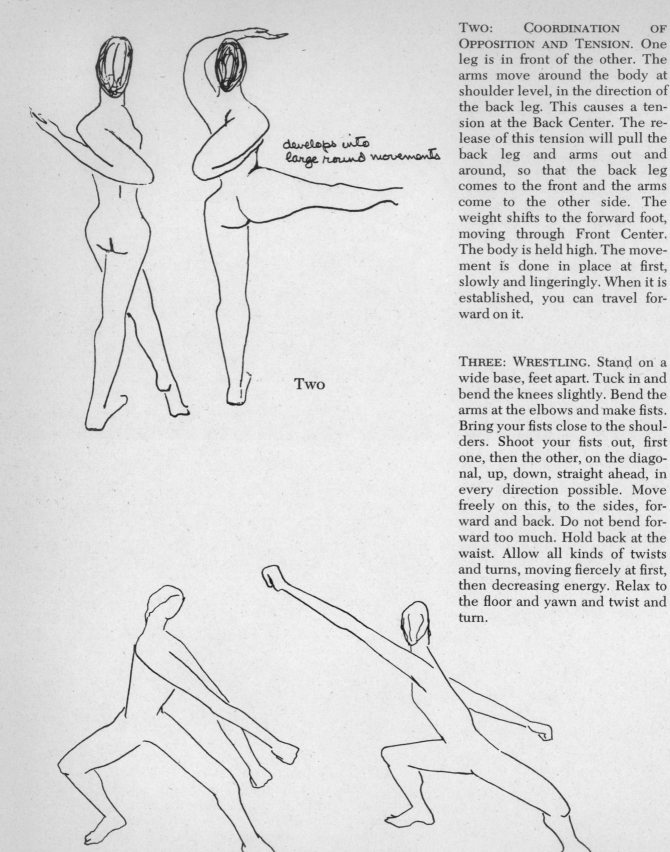

develops into large round movements

Two

THREE: WRESTLING. Stand on a wide base, feet apart. Tuck in and bend the knees slightly. Bend the arms at the elbows and make fists. Bring your fists close to the shoulders. Shoot your fists out, first one, then the other, on the diagonal, up, down, straight ahead, in every direction possible. Move freely on this, to the sides, forward and back. Do not bend forward too much. Hold back at the waist. Allow all kinds of twists and turns, moving fiercely at first, then decreasing energy. Relax to the floor and yawn and twist and turn.

THREE

TWO: COORDINATION OF OPPOSITION AND TENSION. One leg is in front of the other. The arms move around the body at shoulder level, in the direction of the back leg. This causes a tension at the Back Center. The release of this tension will pull the back leg and arms out and around, so that the back leg comes to the front and the arms come to the other side. The weight shifts to the forward foot, moving through Front Center. The body is held high. The movement is done in place at first, slowly and lingeringly. When it is established, you can travel forward on it.

FOUR: THE SNAKE. Lie down flat on your stomach, face turned to the side, and wriggle. Twist the chest up and around to one side and the hips will automatically follow. Turn the chest to the other side. The hips follow, lifting and turning to the same side as the chest. Repeat from side to side, front to back, twisting, lifting and turning, the hips always following the chest.

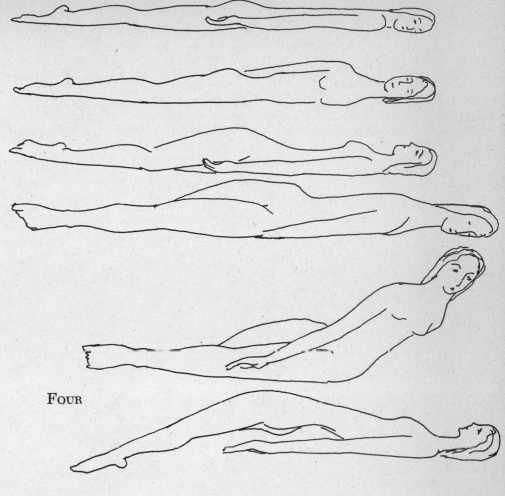

FIVE: Think of your two legs as one—feet together, tuck in, knees slightly bent. Move your knees to the right side, letting the hips follow, then the rib cage, shoulders, head. Relax the body to Center and repeat to the left side.

FOUR

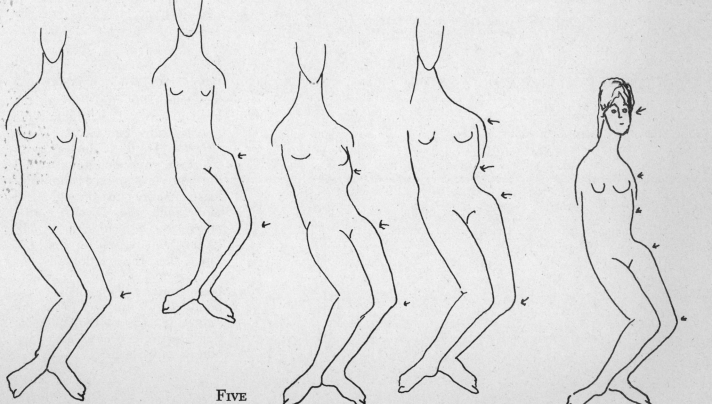

FIVE

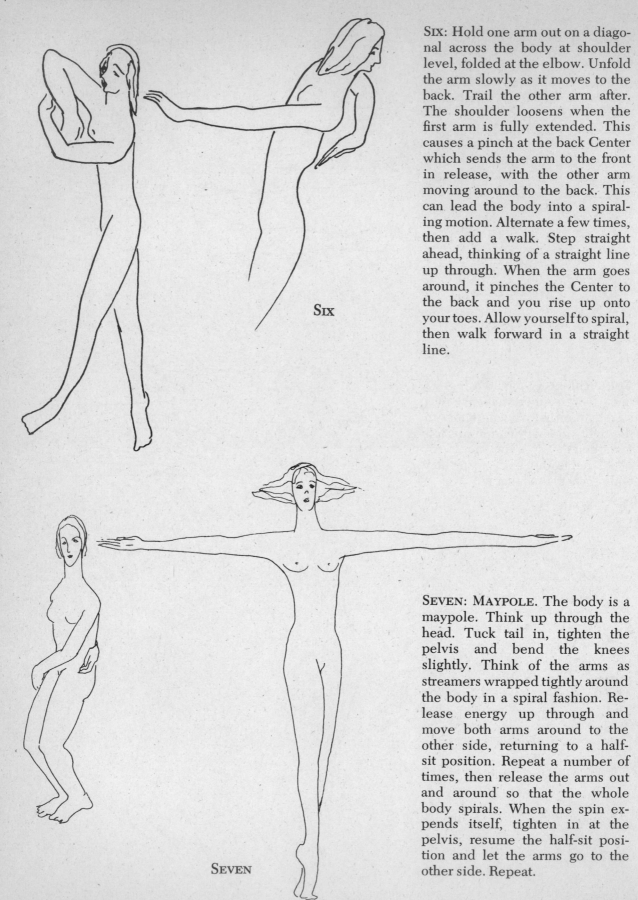

SIX

SEVEN

SIX: Hold one arm out on a diagonal across the body at shoulder level, folded at the elbow. Unfold the arm slowly as it moves to the back. Trail the other arm after. The shoulder loosens when the first arm is fully extended. This causes a pinch at the back Center which sends the arm to the front in release, with the other arm moving around to the back. This can lead the body into a spiraling motion. Alternate a few times, then add a walk. Step straight ahead, thinking of a straight line up through. When the arm goes around, it pinches the Center to the back and you rise up onto your toes. Allow yourself to spiral, then walk forward in a straight line.

SEVEN: MAYPOLE. The body is a maypole. Think up through the head. Tuck tail in, tighten the pelvis and bend the knees slightly. Think of the arms as streamers wrapped tightly around the body in a spiral fashion. Release energy up through and move both arms around to the other side, returning to a half-sit position. Repeat a number of times, then release the arms out and around so that the whole body spirals. When the spin expends itself, tighten in at the pelvis, resume the half-sit position and let the arms go to the other side. Repeat.

Falls, Folds and Unfolds

Think up through the head each time you come up from being folded over. Think of a line that goes through the head and beyond. When extending an arm or leg, think of a line continuing beyond the fingers or toes. During floorwork, after curling yourself around your Center, think of lines extending beyond the head, toes and fingers, or head and toes, depending on the movement.

Falls can help to connect upper and lower body, and also to break up the torso into three parts, upper, middle and lower. Do falls when the body is warm—step, step and then a large step forward; the torso falling over the front knee. Press Down on the front foot and the torso will slowly return upright. At the highest point, let the back leg move forward. Then step, step and a large step forward, and the torso falls over the new front knee.

ONE: HANGING OVER A CLOTHESLINE. Think of the units and spaces of the body. Let the first four units, one after the other, drop over an imaginary clothesline. The knees and ankles give. Then, starting with the ankles, bring all seven units back up into a straight line, one at a time. Think up through. Repeat.

TWO: THE SNAIL. Lie on one side and curl up. Then uncurl head, shoulders, midriff, tail, legs. Turn to other side and curl. Bring legs in first, then tail, then midriff, shoulders and head. Uncurl slowly and turn onto the other side. Repeat.

THREE: A **SCARECROW IN THE WIND.** The scarecrow is hanging from the back Center. The arms are picked up by the wind and flung out, the head following their motion. One leg, then the other, is picked up and flung by the wind. This happens as you stand in place. Concentration on the wind's blowing will eventually lead to a mad, chaotic dance, as if you were being blown and driven by the wind, across the cornfield. The head, arms and legs are flung out from the Center.

THREE

FOUR: **PEARLS DROPPING OFF A STRING.** The head pulls up, moves forward in an arc and hangs heavily. Feel each vertebra pull up, separate itself from the one below and fold over. Do this slowly, down the entire length of the spine.

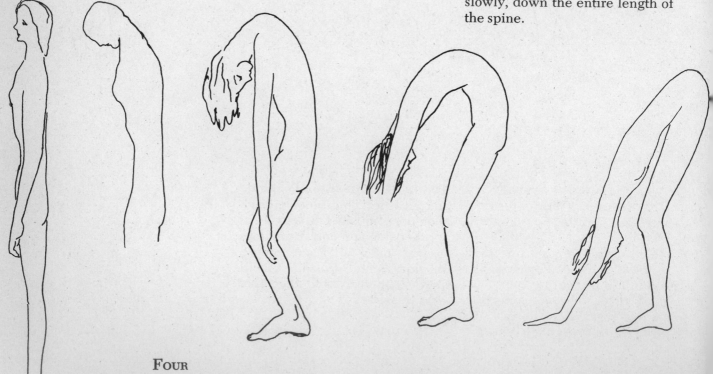

FOUR

FIVE: THE CATERPILLAR CURLING INTO ITSELF. Stand up straight, with tail tucked-in. Drop the head over from the base of the skull. Then stretch each vertebra up and slowly drop it over, one after the other. Bend the knees and ankles until you are all curled into yourself like a caterpillar. Tighten in at the end of the spine as you come slowly up, vertebra by vertebra. When you are all the way up, think higher than the head. This movement can develop into over-arcs.

FIVE

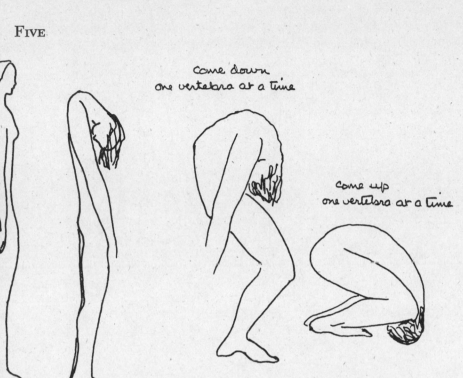

come down one vertebra at a time

come up one vertebra at a time

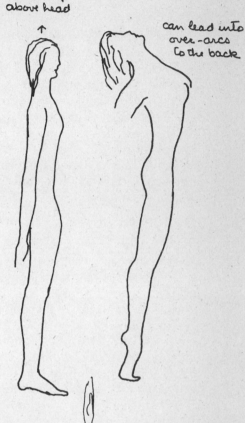

think up above head

can lead into over-arcs to the back

Oppositions

ONE: THE CAT. Tail tucked-in, opposing arm and leg forward. Move shoulder and hip forward, then the elbow and knee, hand and foot, fingers and toes in a stretching and clawing movement. First one arm and leg, then the other. After the pattern is established, stretch and claw high and low, reaching up as far as you can, out at shoulder level, at waist level and down to knee level.

TWO: THE FERRIS WHEEL OR SPIDER WEB. Stand up through, very tall. Raise one arm, keeping the other down close to your body. Bring the leg on the side of the down arm to the front. Stretch up, with your weight on the front foot. Linger on the stretch. Then bring the back leg to the front and the down arm forward and up, as the up arm moves around to the back. Both arms pull from the shoulders. The shoulders pull from the Center. The legs change places on the upward pull. The weight is transferred as the arms begin to change positions.

TWO

THREE: SHIP IN A FOG. One foot in front of the other, stand with the body on a straight line up through. Move one shoulder around to the front. The arm follows and wraps tightly around the body. Move through the Center onto the ball of the front foot. This releases the shoulder and arm out and around toward the back. The other shoulder and arm then take the movement. The circling shoulder and arm are the fog. The body is the tall ship. Move freely. Press your weight against the shoulder girdle to the back and then against the back of the neck. Pulling the chin in helps to do this.

FOUR: Body up-through on a straight line, arms at sides, bent at the elbows. Feet point straight forward, one in front of the other. The shoulder on the side of the front leg and the opposite hip move up and forward. Simultaneously, the other shoulder and hip dip down. Repeat, emphasizing front toes and back heel. This can lead into a spiraling

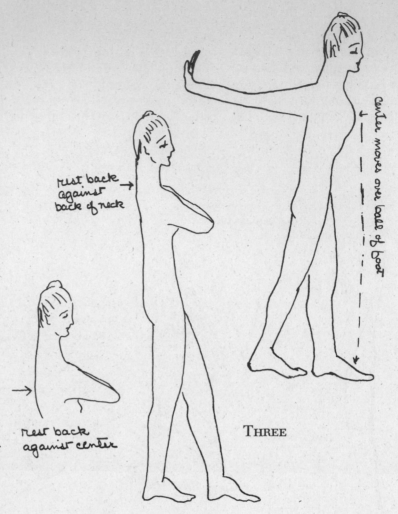

rest back against back of neck

rest back against center

center moves over ball of foot

THREE

movement of the whole body. The movement is slow and formal at first, then light and springy.

FIVE: VASE CARRIERS. Walk with the body tall, thinking up through. Keep your body as slimmed-in as possible with both arms raised and bent at the elbows as if you were carrying a vase on your head. Move opposite leg and shoulder forward. Keep the long vertical line and take small steps forward. After each step, stretch up through the head. This releases the back leg, which dangles forward. The Center moves across the ball of the front foot. Relax slightly, then up through again as opposite shoulder and leg move to the front.

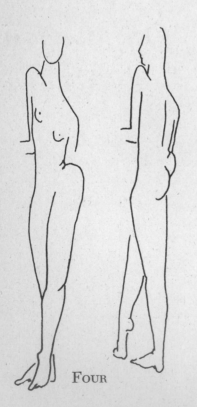

FOUR

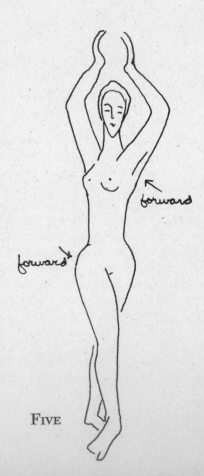

forward

forward

FIVE

SIX: FRICTION OF THE ABDOMINAL WALL. Move one hip up and the shoulder on that side down over it. As the shoulder moves down and to the back, the hip comes up and forward. Alternate sides. Repeat. You should feel a pull from the shoulder joint to the ear.

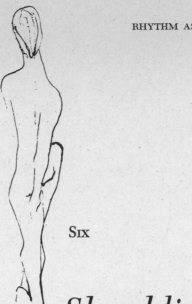

SIX

Shredding and Shaking

A "shred" is done as if something were being thrown or shredded *out*, whereas a "shake" does not have this outward movement, but happens in one place.

ONE: Shake hands, arms, shoulders, feet, legs, hips, first on one side, then the other. Then shake both arms together, then arm and leg on one side, then on the other.

TWO: With feet together, start at the knees and vibrate the entire body. This is done through an inner tension and by concentrating on the idea of vibrating.

Tightening Forces, Resistive Work and Balances

Concentration is on the curled-in end of spine, pulled-in pelvis and strong resistance to the up-through movements.

ONE: Lie flat on your back with knees up and feet flat on the floor. Push your crotch up as high as possible with a strong tuck-in. Rest on your arms. Then, starting with the vertebra just below the neck, slowly lower yourself, vertebra by vertebra, until you are lying flat on the floor again. Press each vertebra to the floor as it comes down. The raised crotch resists the downward pull of the vertebra. When you are completely down, tuck in even harder and draw your navel forcefully down in. Release and repeat. This movement stretches the spaces between the vertebrae.

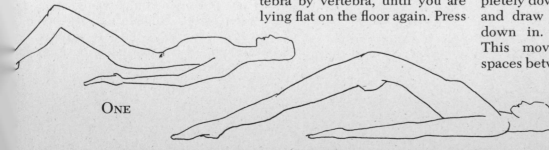

ONE

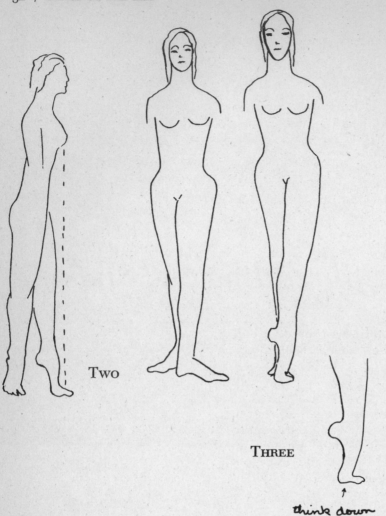

TWO

THREE

TWO: A PLUMB LINE. Turn feet out at a terrific angle, one foot close in front of the other. The Center is over the ball of the front foot. You are forced up through on a balance. The back leg comes around to front, staying close, like a plumb-line string with a weight on it. The leg is the string and the weight is the foot. The Center comes across over the ball of the front foot. Come down on the heel of the front foot with a percussive movement, then up through onto the toes.

THREE: Keeping a strongly tucked-in pelvis, smite the earth with the foot or press the foot down hard and feel the strength mount up into the gripped pelvis. Press down hard through the hips and pelvis.

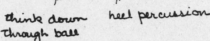

think down through ball heel percussion

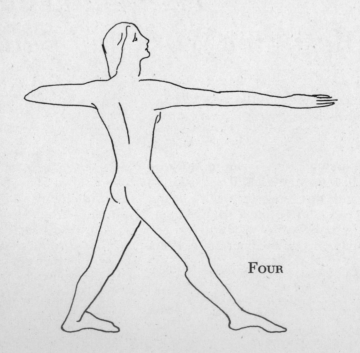

FOUR

FOUR: THE ARROW. The further back the bow is pulled, the further forward the arrow flies. Hold both arms at shoulder level, one arm out straight in front and the other back, bent at the elbow. The leg is forward on the same side as the forward arm. Raise Center high. Draw back with the elbow and resist with the Center. The pull of the forward arm and leg pulls you on forward, step, step, step. Then bring the back arm forward, as the forward arm is pulled to the back position through the elbow.

FIVE

FIVE: Place one foot a comfortable distance in front of the other and bend the back knee. Keep the front leg straight. Pull the elbows back and open the hands, holding them palms forward at shoulder level. Push forward at the Center and with your hands, until the hands are extended as far forward as possible. Bend the front knee and raise the back leg up with the knee straight, so that the body stretches out horizontal. Making fists of your hands, pull them back to the shoulders, where they open out flat, fingers up. The back leg now comes to the front, with a straight knee. The heel comes down first, then the full foot. The bent knee is now in back. It has straightened to let the other leg pass. The pressure forward and the pull backward are done as if against great resistance. Repeat.

SIX: THE CHARIOT. One foot is in front of the other at a comfortable distance with the front knee bent. Move the Center forward as the arms extend to the back. The Center pulls forward against the backward pull of the arms. Then it moves back and the arms pull around to the front. The back knee bends, then step, step, step, as the Center is moving forward. Repeat.

SIX

5

The Lesson Plans

Like the previous exercises, the fifty-three lesson plans that follow are designed to help make your body a fitting instrument for the spirit's use. Each lesson is flexible and does not necessarily have to be carried out exactly as presented. But it is advisable that you follow the overall sequence, one lesson to the next, which is meant, first, to break up the body and make it fluid, and then gradually to strengthen it. You may repeat individual lessons as often as you think necessary, and there may be times when you would like to try them separately as pure techniques. The amount of time taken for each exercise will depend on the purpose of the particular lesson.

Remember to use your imagination and feeling, whether you are teaching or working alone. It is not necessary that you finish a complete lesson plan in one session. You may find that as you do one thing, so many movements evolve from it that you want to stay with that pattern or symbol, giving it a chance to evolve and express itself through your individual rhythmic sense. The more you repeat a pattern, the more you allow your will and mind to relax. The body accepts the pattern, and your own creativity then has a chance to function.

A group of dancers working with a single piece of music might find themselves moving on the same beat, but what flows through each individual could appear very different to an outsider watching. I say "*an outsider* watching" because it is hoped that you, the dancer, are so involved with what is happening within yourself that you could not possibly be watching the rest of the group. Rhythm is a form of meditation and, like all meditative processes, it takes a period of preparation before it begins to work. You must accept the apparent contradiction between externals—lesson plans, forms, techniques— and complete inner concentration. This is something that you will have to work out carefully for yourself. Accept the fact that you are both immortal spirit and physical being. Then it will happen.

Do not be discouraged if you are working alone without a teacher. Follow the lesson plans and you will train your body. Know that you can dance if you have love and patience. This is an exploration into your unknown self. When you are truly involved you will not be self-conscious whether you are by yourself or with a group.

Before you begin, read each lesson through so that you understand it. For certain exercises, specific music is suggested because it has the kind of rhythm, or beat, that the body will respond to most easily. It is generally intended that the choice of music be left to the dancer. Always establish the pattern fully before you do it to music. You will find it interesting to feel the body's responses to the rhythms of various kinds of music, within the same pattern form.

NOTE: The phrase "step, two, three" and all related expressions, mean more than "take three steps" (or whatever). It means take one step and follow it with two steps according to your own feeling.

"Over an arc" (or an over-arc) means being stretched up and then more, as if you were coming over in an arc, to the front or the back or side, depending on the movement pattern.

Unless otherwise specified, always tuck in and relax the knees on a down movement.

"Move on it" means move freely within the pattern.

Lesson Plan One

ONE

ONE: THE JACOB'S LADDER STRETCH. Stand with feet together, heels pressed down, and arms pulled up high. Stretch one arm up, then the other, higher and higher, as if you were climbing a ladder. Continue the pattern for some time, to loosen your body. It will stretch the sides, pull the ribs up and lift the chest.

TWO: With one foot in front of the other, feel your breastbone Center, front and back, with your hands to get a sense of its exact location. Drop your hands to your sides and concentrate on your Center. Think that you are being pushed at the Center from back to front. This may bring you onto your toes or move you a few steps ahead. When the movement forward has expended itself, think that you are being pushed from the front Center to the back. It is most important to concentrate on the feeling of being pushed. Continue doing this for a long time, being pushed first to the front and then to the back. You will find yourself being moved quite far in both directions. The head and arms will become involved, following the lead of the Center. When the pattern is fully established, accompany it with music that has big, circular movements. Now move freely, but with head, arms and feet always following the Center.

THREE: Think of the seven units. Starting with the head, move each unit as if separating it from the rest of the body. Let it arc over forward and hang down. Move down to the floor, and up and down a number of times, dropping the units off and putting them back on. End on the floor.

FOUR: Rest on your side, all curled in, head and knees touching. On an impulse, stretch out on your back, with head, arms and legs extended. Roll to the other side and curl in.

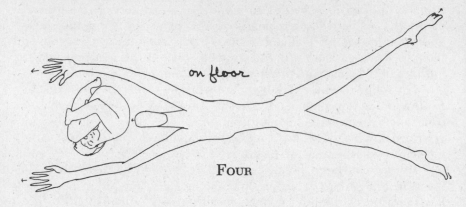

on floor

FOUR

FIVE: Rest on your back, stretching softly and thinking of rootlets stretching underground.

SIX: Raise one hip and move it up and over until you roll over onto your face. Then carry the movement through with the other hip and roll over again, going in the same direction. Roll down the length of the room, then back to the other end, the hip always leading and the upper torso following.

SEVEN: THE SICKLE MOON. Free movement in form. Start with the feet together. Hold the arms to the right side at shoulder height, and move them down and up on the left side, down and up on the right, and then down around and up over the head and down the right side to come up on the left. Keep repeating the pattern—half-circle, half-circle, circle, and then half-circle—until the pattern is established. Keep your body relaxed. The legs, feet and head will enter into the movement. Use waltz music.

Lesson Plan Two

ONE: THE JACOB'S LADDER STRETCH.

TWO: For space at the wrist, circle the hand from the wrist—around, up, out, down. Then, for space at the elbow, raising your arm to shoulder level, circle the forearm from the elbow—up, out and down. For space at the shoulder, using the entire arm, circle in, up, out and down from the shoulder. Relax the arm, then circle the shoulder toward the Center, up, around and back toward the back Center and down. Repeat each movement a number of times before going on. Then do them in a continuous flowing sequence. First move the shoulder from the Center, up, around toward the back Center and down. Circle entire arm from the shoulder, in, up out, around to the back and down. Raising the arm to shoulder height, move the forearm in toward the underarm, up and out at shoulder height. Then circle the hand from the wrist, down, around, up and out. Repeat the sequence and then do it on the other side. Then move both sides together, until there is one continuous movement. Allow the head to become involved. Repeat. Then do the same with the feet at the ankles, legs to the knees, thighs to hips. You can vary this exercise by making it a circle, a fold and unfold, or a shred (i.e., a shaking out).

THREE: Relax the body and let it droop forward from the hips. Become an elephant moving through the forest, swaying your arms from side to side as if they were a trunk. The weight swinging over to one side frees the opposite leg to move forward.

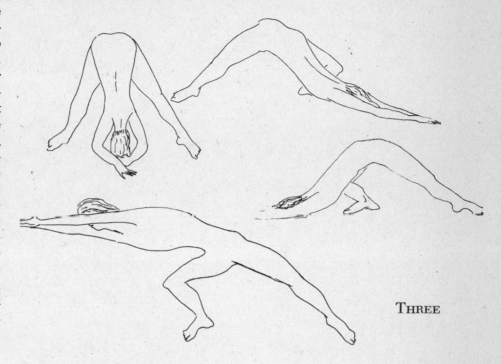

THREE

FOUR: SOFT SAND. Lie on the floor, back pressed flat so that all vertebrae touch the floor. Then, pointing the toes, shoot the legs up, first one at a time, then both together. This lifts the lower torso off floor. The element of surprise is useful in breaking down bodily resistance.

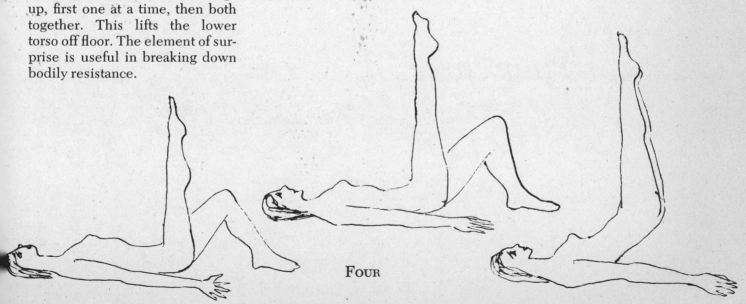

FOUR

FIVE: Lie on your side and draw the body together. Roll over onto your knees, bring one knee up and put the foot on the floor, then the other foot as you unfold up as high as you can. Crumple to the floor and come up again. Repeat a number of times.

FIVE

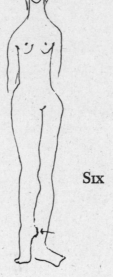

SIX: SPARKLES ON THE WATER. Standing with feet together, move the heels up and down one at a time, until you feel light and high in the chest, with feet dancing delicately.

SIX

Lesson Plan Three

ONE: THE JACOB'S LADDER STRETCH.

TWO: Stand with feet together, tail well tucked-in. Thinking of units and spaces, fold and unfold the body slowly, logically, down and up.

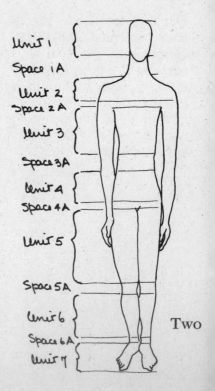

Unit 1
Space 1A
Unit 2
Space 2A
Unit 3
Space 3A
Unit 4
Space 4A
Unit 5
Space 5A
Unit 6
Space 6A
Unit 7

TWO

THREE: THE WATER CARRIER. Imagine you have a heavy bucket of water in each hand. The weight of the buckets pulls first one arm down, then the other. The body stretches upward through the head as the arms pull down. The neck becomes very long, stretching at the sides from ear to shoulder.

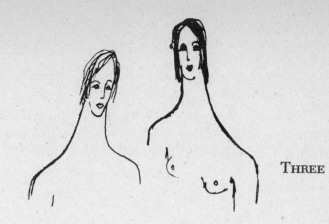

THREE

FOUR: THE ELEPHANT. (See page 39)

FIVE: Lie down on your side, with head, knees and arms drawn together in a ball. Breathe deeply into the lower lungs. Roll onto your back with all five points—head, arms and legs—extended and spread. Then roll to the other side and into a ball. Repeat a few times and then roll onto your knees and stand up. Stretch up as high as possible and crumple to the floor. From starting position, repeat the stretch and fall several times.

SIX: Stand with one foot in front of the other. Think up through the head. Step, two, three, feet together and jump three times. Continue stepping and jumping. When tired, step slowly and raise the heels three times instead of jumping. Let the arms come into it, and the movement develop into turns. Continue to think up through the head and Center.

Lesson Plan Four

ONE: THE JACOB'S LADDER STRETCH.

TWO: You are a scarecrow on a pole. The wind shakes your arms and legs. Shake the hands from the wrists until you lose all sense of your fingers. The scarecrow has stuffing: think of the stuffing being shaken out. After shaking the hands down from the wrists, shake the forearm from the elbow, then the whole arm from the shoulder. Shake one arm first, then the other, then both to-

gether. Think of gusts of wind picking the arms up and shaking them, letting them drop, then picking them up and shaking them again. The arm shoots out and shakes from the Center. The Center rebounds up. Do the same with the ankles, knees, hips, shaking out the stuffing. Then feel as if the whole leg is being shaken out from the Center. Complete one leg, then the other. This exercise can be used as a shred or a shake in one lesson and a circular movement in another. A circular shoulder movement can lead to a

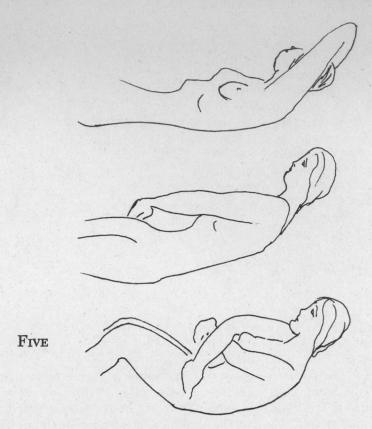

machine motion. Use your imagination and develop the movement according to your needs and the time of the year—e.g., shake out all the winter congestion.

THREE: One leg is picked up by the wind and shaken, from hip to knee to ankle, out to the side. It falls with the heel down to meet the other heel. The harder the fall the greater the upward rebound of the other leg. Continue for a while until tired, then continue lethargically until the energy wells up again.

FOUR: Feel the body being blown across the field. It is blown around until all the stuffing is gone. The body sinks to the floor like a heap of rags. The rags are picked up by the wind, blown around, swept up into a straight line and dropped to the floor. Continue until you are warm and tired. Relax to the floor with a sense of weightlessness. The body is pulsing, emptying and filling. Rest on your back, softly, sleepily.

FIVE

FIVE: Still lying on the floor, move one arm in a circle softly around the head as the shoulder lifts from the floor. Put stress in the downward movement. Circle with one arm for a while, then with the other. Then with both arms together. It should lead into a pelvic rock. As the arms move downward, the head will move back.

SIX: Relax, roll over onto your knees and come up slowly into a soft walking movement, arms and legs going forward in opposition.

SEVEN: With legs apart, arms out at shoulder level, swing the right leg up to its own side and then swing the right leg and arm down, across and up to the other side. As this happens, turn and leap. At first it is a half-turn, then it becomes a full turn. Think of your legs as turning from a high center, and as being very long. Repeat with the left leg.

SEVEN

Lesson Plan Five

This lesson is more restrained than the previous one, as it stresses rest in movement, action in inaction. The scarecrow remains on the pole. It is not blown about. It is being moved as in a lullaby.

ONE: THE JACOB'S LADDER STRETCH.

TWO: Shred out hands, arms, feet, legs.

THREE: A version of the scarecrow. Pull arms forward to shoulder height from back Center. The head follows. Pull arms forward a number of times and allow head to follow. Then pull the head forward from the back Center and let the arms follow the movement of the head. The head comes up and the arms come down. Then let the head go and allow a small reflected movement to happen at the Center. Think of soft breezes blowing, moving head and arms gently to the front. When the breeze stops, the head rises and the arms fall back to the lowered position. Think of an up-breath coming from the Center. The head rises and falls on it.

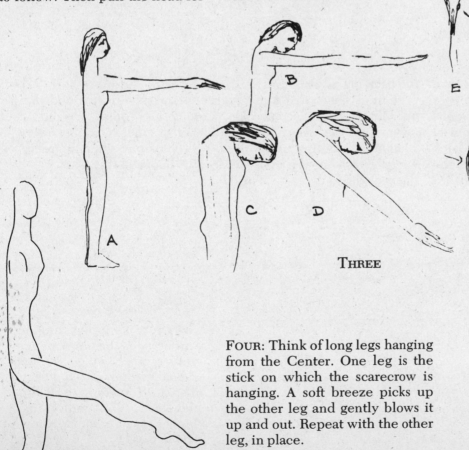

THREE

FOUR: Think of long legs hanging from the Center. One leg is the stick on which the scarecrow is hanging. A soft breeze picks up the other leg and gently blows it up and out. Repeat with the other leg, in place.

FOUR

FIVE: Think of a wind blowing horizontally so that the ribcage is raised on one side and the upper chest section leans over to the other side. Feel the pinch at your waist. The wind comes under the armpit and blows shoulder and arm to the other side, where the arm hangs heavily. The heavier it hangs, the more lightly it will rebound up. Concentrate on getting the back of the lungs to breathe up, which will lift the shoulder and arm. It feels like a rebound from the heaviness. The wind now blows on an even stronger horizontal, from one side and then the other. Feel that the chest is being lifted round and high, setting up a small beat or vibration that moves the head, arms and one leg in any direction—back, front, sideways, up or down.

FIVE

SIX: THE DISCUS THROWER. One leg takes a large step in front of the other. The front knee bends and the torso is pulled up, out of the hips. Press down on the back heel and against the back of the back knee. Twist the torso toward the back leg as you bend forward over front knee. Bring the arms up and back to that side. Press down on the front foot and straighten, feeling a line of energy come up through. Circle the back leg to the front. Turn the torso to the other side, carrying the arms with it. Bend the front knee and repeat. Do this a number of times, coming over as low as possible. Finally, relax onto the floor and rest.

SEVEN: Stand up, thinking up through the head. With feet together, raise and lower one heel, then the other, very light and fast. Think of dewdrops sparkling on the grass. This will bring you higher and higher on your toes, and taller.

SIX

Lesson Plan Six

ONE: Stand tall with feet together. Stretch one arm up past the other in the Jacob's Ladder stretch. Keep the heels down. Continue until body is well stretched-out.

TWO: SPRING AWAKENS THE SCARECROW. Your head, coatsleeves, and pant legs are stuffed with straw. The right hand is at the Center. Move it to the left shoulder and down the left arm to the fingertips. Imagine that you are following the movement of straw leaking out from joint to joint. Do this three or four times to one side, then to the other. Reach over your shoulder to back Center and then move the hand up to the head. Do this with one hand, then the other, repeating three or four times with each hand. Move the hand from front Center to the top of the head in a similar manner, first one hand, then the other, three or four times each. Move the hand from the Center down one leg to the ankle, back up and down the other leg, and up again to Center. Do this three or four times with each hand. One leg, then the other, moves up softly and then comes down. Imagine that a brisk wind is blowing the trouser leg up high. Do this for a long time. The arms rise with the upward movement.

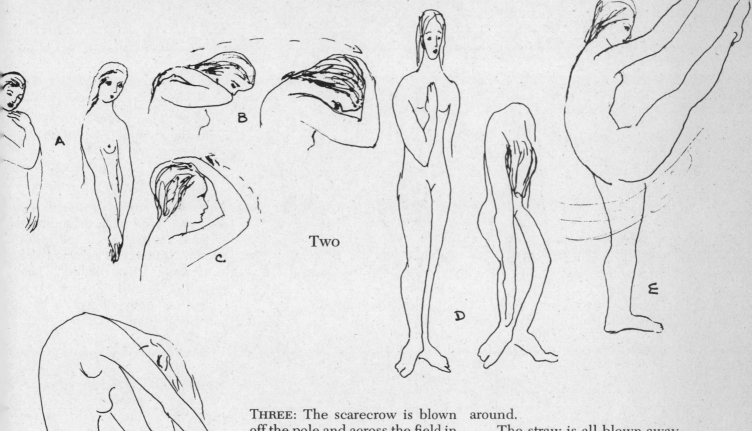

Two

THREE: The scarecrow is blown off the pole and across the field in a big, circular motion, propelled from the back Center, cross the room in a free, reeling movement. As wind dies down, you are dropped to the ground, only to be picked up again and blown around.

The straw is all blown away. The rags (body) lie on the ground (floor). The soft snow comes, covering the ground and swirling around the scarecrow. The body rests on its side, curled up now to keep warm. All is motionless.

THREE

FOUR: Spring comes. The earth cracks open. Stretch out on one side and then curl up again. Stretch out and curl on each side three or four times. Roll back and forth from side to side, then roll over onto your knees and stand up.

FIVE: The Spring grasses and little flowers are growing. Your heels feel very sprightly. Keeping toes on the floor, lift one heel as high as possible. As it goes down, the other heel comes up. Feel bouncy and joyous. Think of the sunlight and air of spring.

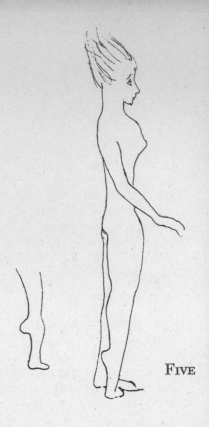

FIVE

Lesson Plan Seven

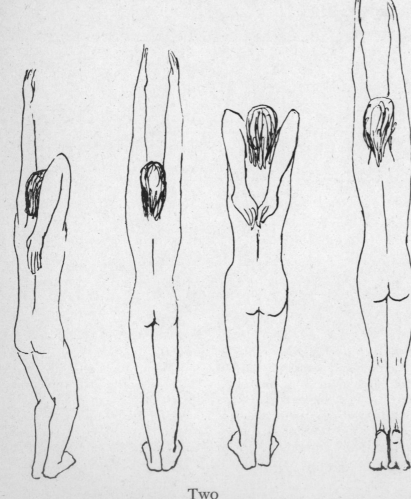

TWO

ONE: THE JACOB'S LADDER STRETCH. Then stretch up and up. Relax the shoulders and then repeat the stretch.

TWO: With arms stretched up, drop one hand back from elbow to back Center. Keep the other arm up. Stretch it. Alternate sides until body feels pliable. Then stretch both arms together. Drop both arms from elbows to back and bring them up and stretch. Repeat.

THREE: Think of the way a puppeteer moves puppets around in space, down and up. The puppet is pulled up high from back Center and then let go, so that it falls to the floor on its side, limp. It is pulled up again at back Center. Come up on toes as arms stretch up. Come down on heels as arms drop. Then alternate heel and

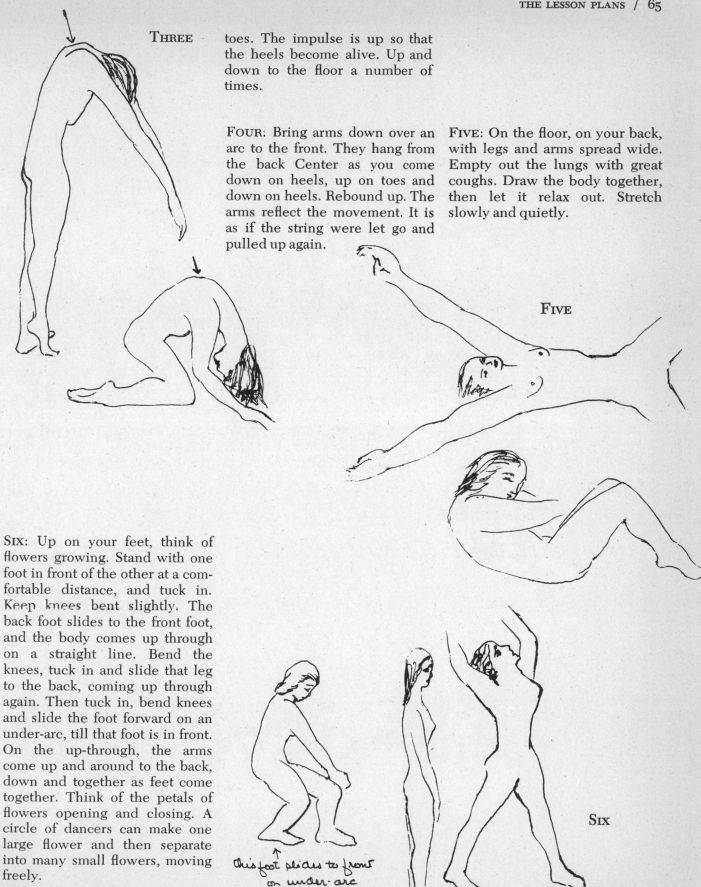

THREE · toes. The impulse is up so that the heels become alive. Up and down to the floor a number of times.

FOUR: Bring arms down over an arc to the front. They hang from the back Center as you come down on heels, up on toes and down on heels. Rebound up. The arms reflect the movement. It is as if the string were let go and pulled up again.

FIVE: On the floor, on your back, with legs and arms spread wide. Empty out the lungs with great coughs. Draw the body together, then let it relax out. Stretch slowly and quietly.

FIVE

SIX: Up on your feet, think of flowers growing. Stand with one foot in front of the other at a comfortable distance, and tuck in. Keep knees bent slightly. The back foot slides to the front foot, and the body comes up through on a straight line. Bend the knees, tuck in and slide that leg to the back, coming up through again. Then tuck in, bend knees and slide the foot forward on an under-arc, till that foot is in front. On the up-through, the arms come up and around to the back, down and together as feet come together. Think of the petals of flowers opening and closing. A circle of dancers can make one large flower and then separate into many small flowers, moving freely.

this foot slides to front on under-arc

SIX

Lesson Plan Eight

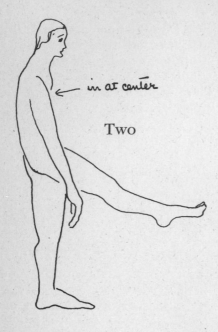

in at center

TWO

TWO: Press Center in. Tuck in tail and release one leg up. It drops, and the Center comes up. Alternate. Repeat many times.

THREE: DOLL SYMBOL. Say "mama," mechanically, as a doll would. This grips the stomach in. One leg swings up as the pelvis rocks forward. Alternate legs. The movement starts slowly, then quickens, and then slows down again. The arms will become involved. The slowing down is movement in rest.

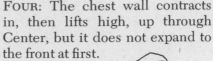

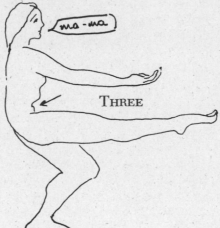

ma-ma

THREE

FOUR: The chest wall contracts in, then lifts high, up through Center, but it does not expand to the front at first.

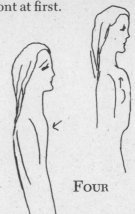

FOUR

ONE: A parallel line stretch. Stretch both arms up together so that it pulls you onto your toes. Then concentrate on lifting the chest wall. Feel it so high that it floats. Release at shoulders, but keeping the arms up. This will bring you down from your toes.

FIVE: Move on it, bringing the feet down hard. Strike with the heel. Keep the chin in. Bring both arms and one leg forward, leading with the heels of the hands and with the heels of the feet. When the heel hits the floor the Center moves strongly forward, sending the head, arms and back leg flying out backward.

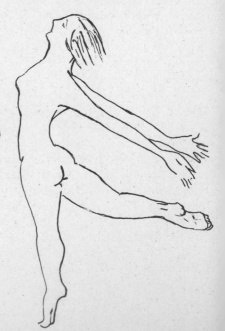

FIVE

SIX: THE SUN IS GOING DOWN.
One foot is in front of the other in
a comfortably wide position. The
body pulls out of the hips and
bends forward and the front knee
bends until the Center is over the
front knee, and the knee is above
the ball of the foot. Press down
on the front foot, which will cause
the torso to come up as the line
moves up through. The back leg
comes to the front. Repeat.

SEVEN: After a while, on the up-
through, the Center turns toward
the back leg, the body follows the
turn, and you step, two, three. Repeat the turn first to one side,
then to the other.

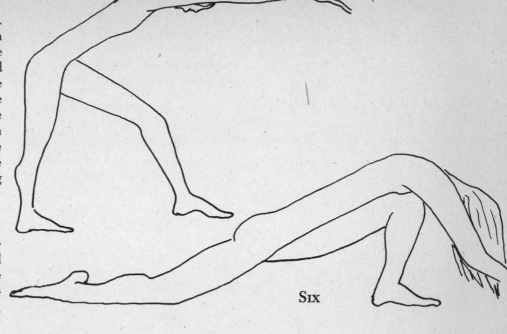

Six

EIGHT: THE SUN IS MOVING
ACROSS THE SKY. As you turn,
move across the room and come
down over the front knee as in
Six. Stand up and turn and move
quite freely, while maintaining
the pattern of bending, moving
and turning. Then, when tired,
lie down on the floor.

NINE: Lie on your side in a long
line from head to toes. Stretch the
bottom arm out. Bend the top arm
at the elbow, so that the hand
rests on the floor in front of you.
Stretch the top leg and bend the
bottom leg at the knee, drawing
the knee up toward the chest.
Raise the top leg, stretching
through the big toe. The head
comes up to meet it. This exerts
a terrific pinch at the under arm,
which draws up to a comfortable
place. Then lower the leg and extend arm in a long horizontal
stretch. Repeat a number of
times, stretching up and down.
Turn, toward the back stretching
softly, to the other side. The top
arm comes over the head and the
lower arm moves up and over. Repeat stretching up and down on
the other side.

SEVEN

NINE

TEN: Draw together and roll over onto your knees. The Center is flattened down forward and raised up a number of times. Come up onto your feet.

ELEVEN: THE SUN IS SPARKLING ON THE WATER. Standing tall, lift one heel up, then the other. Alternate in very light and high,

sparkling movements. Go so quickly you lose track of raising and lowering opposite heels and toes.

TWELVE: Move both arms up and down from one side to the other. They are whitecaps. Move freely with it.

TEN

Lesson Plan Nine

ONE: THE JACOB'S LADDER STRETCH.

TWO: WIND THROUGH A WILLOW TREE. Think of wind blowing from behind you. It starts as gusts and then becomes sustained. Your leg and arms swing up, drop down and are blown up again. Alternate legs. Then the head is blown forward. The long wind sustains the lift of legs and arms.

THREE: You are thrown into a pelvic rock. The chest flattens to the back; the back of the lungs becomes inflated. Repeat again and again. Think of wind coming from the front, blowing into the Center and pelvis. Make a "swish" sound with your breath. Arms and legs swing gently to the front.

FOUR: The wind blows the Center forward and the rest of the body is flung violently to the back. Hold before dropping. Repeat.

FIVE: Feet together, toes pointed out. The wind blows one arm (willow branch) up. Lean out into that underarm. Drop and repeat. Repeat to other side.

SIX: Keep the hip of the supporting leg in as the arms and the free leg are blown out with a swish to the side. Think of the underarm as you lean out as far as possible. Hold the position, drop and repeat to that side for some time, then to the other side. The wind shapes trees according to its prevalent direction.

FIVE

out
under arm

hip
in ⟶

SIX

SEVEN: Swing one leg and both arms out to the same side. The head follows the movement. The leg falls back down to standing and head and arms follow as the other leg swings out to the other side. Very active swinging movement. When tired, think up through head, and then move in a small, high, sustained over-arc from side to side, bringing the leg up only a little. Large, fast springy movements change to a small continuous one, then large and fast again, alternating. Repeat.

SEVEN

EIGHT: Imagine walking on a tightrope with a parasol held high in one hand. Feel the inner borders of the feet. One foot in front of the other, tuck in, knees slightly bent. Feel the rope carefully with the heel, the flat of the foot and the ball. The back leg steals forward and is carefully placed on rope.

EIGHT

NINE: Spread feet apart. Keeping tucked-in with knees bent, jump in quarter-turns for a while, then half turns, then full turns. After each jump, settle into the lower back so that it expands out. The tightening of the buttocks is the pick-up for the next jump. The body lifts from under the buttocks in a springy movement.

NINE

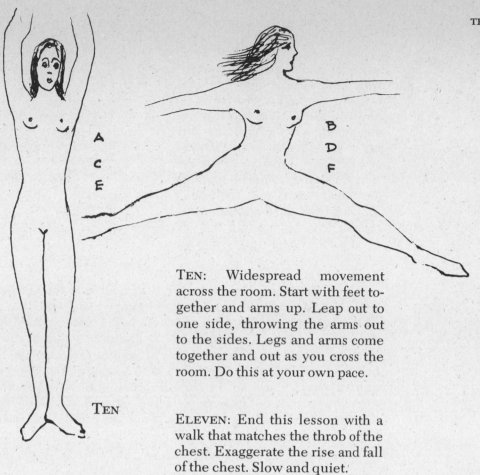

TEN: Widespread movement across the room. Start with feet together and arms up. Leap out to one side, throwing the arms out to the sides. Legs and arms come together and out as you cross the room. Do this at your own pace.

TEN

ELEVEN: End this lesson with a walk that matches the throb of the chest. Exaggerate the rise and fall of the chest. Slow and quiet.

Lesson Plan Ten

ONE: Stand with an erect spine. Parallel stretch up through the arms. Establish the expansion of the chest. Stretch up both sides and let go. Repeat.

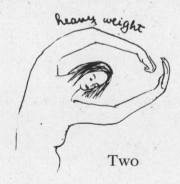

heavy weight

TWO

TWO: Arms up, over-arc from side to side. Feel the pinch under your arm. Feel the upper arm as being very heavy. Think up through your head to get the over-arc.

THREE: Over-arc from side to side from the waist. Keep the knees straight. Do not sink down. Think of waves rolling a ship from one side to the other.

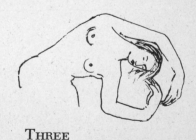

THREE

FOUR

FOUR: Then the arms and head move around and down to the front, arching over from back Center. One leg falls across the other and you are moved two or three steps to the side. Continue a rolling-ship motion from side to side, two or three steps in each direction, bringing arms up, around and down each time. The chest remains high during these movements.

FIVE: The movement and rhythm quicken. Think of the waves as being light and breaking quickly. Then slow down. The feet continue the pattern of moving two or three steps from side to side. Stop and feel a high, soft inhalation of the breath on the up-through each time before you move to the other side. Stay on this a long time.

SIX

SIX: Feel as if the ship were in a storm and you were being thrown around. Tuck in. One leg swings up, bent at the knee, and crosses in front of the other leg. It comes down heavily. Put all your weight on it. Continue for some time in one direction, then the other. Feel more and more unsteady on your feet.

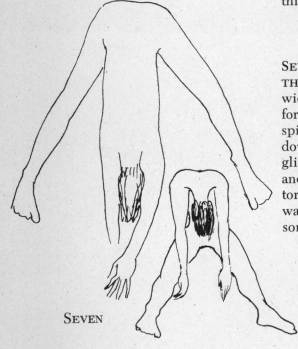

SEVEN

SEVEN: SEAWEED IS MOVED BY THE WAVES. Stand with the legs wide apart and the torso dropped forward from the end of the spine. The torso moves up and down, the head and arms dangling from it. Think of the head and arms as seaweeds, while the torso moves up and down as waves. Continue up and down for some time.

EIGHT: Bending over from the hips swing the torso from side to side. Let your head and arms follow the swing. They have no movement of their own, but are swung by the torso. You can think of them as being moved by the action of the water. This can lead into large, circular movements. Drop to the floor.

NINE: Lie on the floor, face down, arms extended forward. Think of seals on the beach or on rocks. Their black, shining backs glisten as the sun shines down. One shoulder, then arm, elbow, wrist come up and go down. Then the other side does the same. It is very like a swimming motion. Up and down, one arm, then the other, a number of times.

NINE

TEN: The head rises up from Center. Fold your arms in front of you and rest on them. Open your eyes wide. Look at the sand right below you, in front of you. Then look at the water, the horizon and up into the sky. Let your gaze return from the sky to the horizon, the water and back down to the sand. Repeat a number of times.

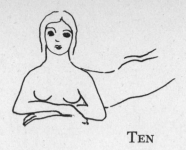

TEN

ELEVEN: Close your eyes and rest your forehead on the floor. Turn your head to one side and open the eyes wide. A cloud is on the horizon. Look at it, wide-eyed. The arms have been out to the front while the eyes were closed; now they move back and fold in under the breast. Rest on your forearms as you follow the movement of the cloud up and around overhead, down the other side and back up, around and down to the side where it started. Now look at the horizon, close your eyes, drop your head and stretch your arms out in front of you. Repeat from the other side. Do this a number of times.

TWELVE: With straight elbows, walk your arms back from the stretched-out position until they are directly under you, lifting you up. Walk them out again and repeat a number of times. Then come onto knees in a folded position and stand.

TWELVE

THIRTEEN: High, tall and light, heels and toes delicately dancing.

Lesson Plan Eleven:

ONE: Start with the parallel line stretch, then over an arc from side to side. See Lesson Plan Ten, Exercise Two.

TWO: As you stretch to the side, let one leg fall across the other and move in the same direction as the stretch. Stretch the arm strongly. Quicken the pace and run, legs side-cutting into space. Think of the north wind blowing low clouds across the sky.

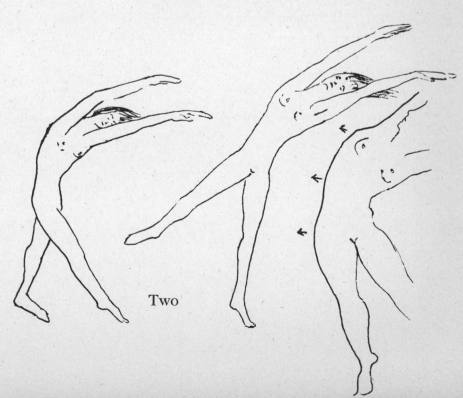

TWO

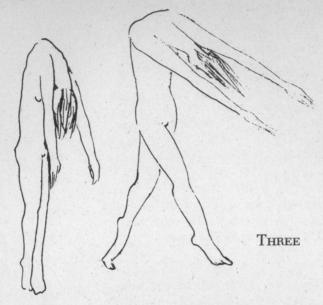

THREE

THREE: Think of the head, arms and legs as meeting at the Center, where they are caught like seaweed on a rock. Let the head hang over from the Center so that it feels as long as the arms. The tide comes in and loosens the seaweed slightly. With the head and arms still hanging limp, move up and down slightly. Think of the peaks of shallow waves moving up the back Center. Breathe with their rhythmic movement. Up and down. Continue this breathing for some time.

FOUR: Feel the tide move the seaweed (hanging head and arms) from side to side. The movement is slight to start. Then it becomes stronger, as if the seaweed had finally been torn loose from the rocks. Let yourself go and move in half-turns. Suggested music—Wagner's Prelude to *Das Rheingold* or "Siegfried's Idyll."

FIVE: The seaweed now floats softly and quietly on the ocean. You are tired. The head relaxes over and then coils in. The knees give and sink, down to the bottom of the sea. Relax onto your side. Imagine seashells, and the soft protoplasmic life inside the hinged shell, moving against it. Slowly roll over onto your knees. Move one side up, then the other side, until you are standing on the knees, head and arms hanging from the Center. Then move down, leading with one side, then the other, until you are back in a crouching position. Move up and down, up and down, until the back feels free (the shell is off). Move freely. The whole back moves with one, then the other side moving continuously, come up to standing, down and up again.

FIVE

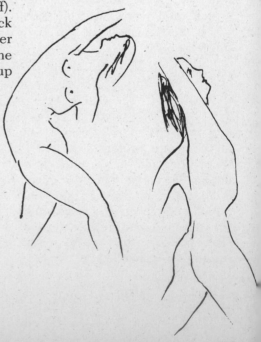

Six: THE SOFT MIST RISES. It comes up slowly, softly, softly. The opposite arm and leg cross. Begin with one foot in front of the other, your weight on the front foot. Then let the back leg and opposing arm come to the front, crossing. Move the other arm to the back until you feel a pinch at the back. Repeat.

SEVEN: Move to the back with buttocks curled under, one foot in front of the other. Fall into the lower back, two, three. Up through on the back foot, then half-sit and repeat, many times.

Six

SEVEN

Lesson Plan Twelve

ONE: The parallel line stretch begins the lesson.

TWO: Shake hands from the wrists, then shred the forearm from the elbow and the entire arm from the shoulder. Shoot an arm and shoulder out from the Center, one arm a number of times, then the other, and then both together. Shake one foot from the ankle, then shred the lower leg from the knee and the whole leg out from the hip. Think of the high Center and shoot your leg out from there, first one leg a number of times and then the other. Raise one leg up to the side, folded at the knee. Shoot it out to the side and allow it to fall down close to the other leg, which then raises and shoots out. Tuck in as the leg drops. Emphasize the down motion and the other leg will rebound up and

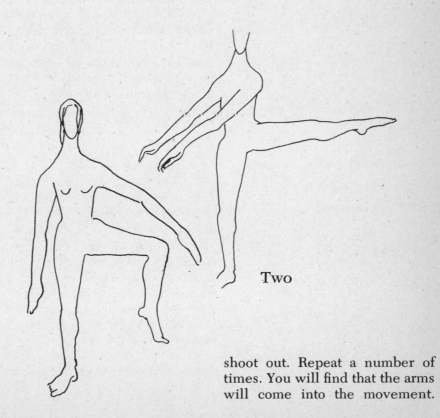

Two

shoot out. Repeat a number of times. You will find that the arms will come into the movement.

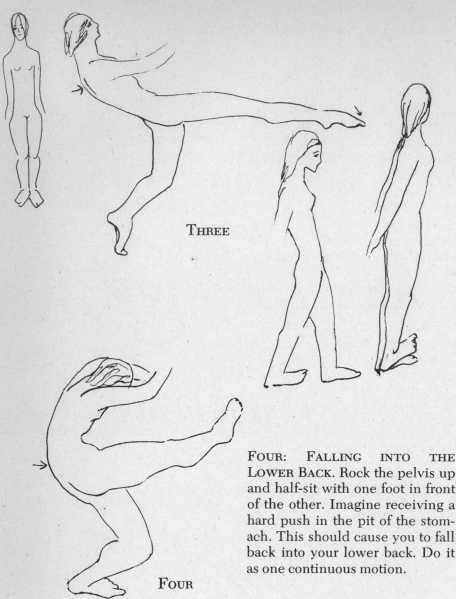

THREE: A long leg swings forward from back Center and falls hard, its heel clicking against the heel of the standing foot. Emphasize the pull of the big toe on the swing up. The leg falls back heavier each time, so that you begin to fall backward a few steps. When the leg falls down and as you are moved backward, feel the percussive beat of the heels, heel, heel. First the percussion is in one place, at the heels, and then in the steps falling back. Spiral backward and then begin to circle. Start with larger circles, then gradually make them smaller and smaller.

FOUR: FALLING INTO THE LOWER BACK. Rock the pelvis up and half-sit with one foot in front of the other. Imagine receiving a hard push in the pit of the stomach. This should cause you to fall back into your lower back. Do it as one continuous motion.

FIVE: Swing one leg loosely back and forth to a definite beat. Swing one leg for a while, then the other, letting the weight shift so that you are picked up off the standing leg. The arms move in the opposite direction to the swinging leg. Waltz music is suggested.

SIX: Two persons hold hands, facing each other, with one leg forward. Holding hands, bend the knees and slowly go down until the buttocks touch the floor. Come up, pushing forward at the crotch, using each other partially as resistance and partially as support. When up, let go hands but stay facing. Let your arms go back and your chest walls meet. Back feet come to the front. Take hands again and go down and up a few times. End down.

SEVEN: On the floor, stretch out on one side with heels together, as if you were a mermaid. Stretch the body out. Extend the bottom arm and hand. Relaxed, the top arm falls comfortably in front of the body. (A) Think of a stretch from the Center. The Center comes up, drawing in the bottom arm, and the head dangles down on a long neck. Then the arm slips out and back down. (B) Move up and down three times. On the third time up, raise the Center higher and lift the top arm up toward the horizon. (C) Move the arm on up toward the sky and around to settle for a moment in back, letting the eyes follow, before returning it to the front. (D) Do this three times to one side and then to the other side.

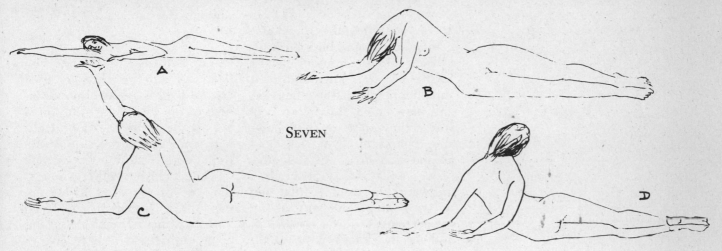

SEVEN

EIGHT: Come up to a sitting height, but stay on your side. Straighten the bottom arm so that it is partially supporting your weight. (A) Move the free arm slowly in a large over-arc toward the sky and down to the back. It stays there. The eyes follow the movement. (B) Then the head slowly turns to the other arm, which now comes up, slowly moving skyward and over to the floor on the other side. The eyes follow the movement. The hips roll over slowly. (C) Repeat to one side and then the other a number of times. Then move in one direction to the end of the room and back.

NINE: Stand up, dance freely. Think high.

EIGHT

Lesson Plan Thirteen

ONE: Start with Jacob's Ladder stretch.

TWO: Heels together, feet at a comfortable angle, both arms out to one side at shoulder height. Swing the arms down and up to shoulder height on the other side, and then down and up to back where they started. Then down and around up over the head, around and down to the other shoulder. Do this until the arms are warm and tired, so that they will respond passively to positive leg movement. Be sure to tuck in, and let the knees go with the movement.

THREE: Then with one foot in front of the other and the weight on front foot, think up through the head so that the back leg can dangle around to the front. Let the heel come down first, then rise on your toes on the next up-through. Repeat.

FOUR: With feet turned out, one foot in front of the other, go down on the back heel and move the heel of the front foot in to touch the big toe of the back foot. Hold both arms out to the side of the front foot. Rest into your back. Now, feet close together, circle to the side of the front foot, step, two, three, around to the back. Weight is on the front foot at the count of three, and the front heel is touching the back big toe. Back leg moves around to the front. Weight is now on the back foot. Settle into the back. Move the arms to the other side on the up-through. Repeat, reversing direction.

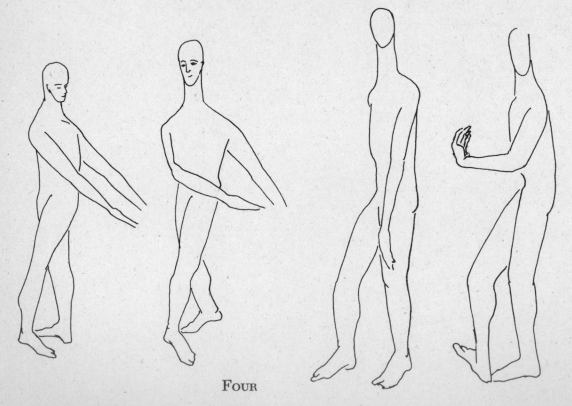

FOUR

terrific shoulder pinch

becomes large movement

FIVE

FIVE: Continue, but with large, formal movements, keeping very high in the chest.

SIX: A CHARLIE CHAPLIN WALK. With feet very turned out, arms and elbows move in opposition to hips. Exaggerate all movements.

SIX

SEVEN: Force breath out with a strong *HA* sound. Move lungs deep down as if into the pit of the stomach. Let the new breath rush in without conscious effort. Flatten the stomach against the back and expand lower back. Exhale again. The movement will lead into a sustained fall into the lower back, then to uncontrolled falls that you can develop into circular backward movements. Recover on the up-breath.

SEVEN

EIGHT: Lie on your back, with head and knees meeting and arms around knees. Rock from side to side, ironing out the back.

NINE: Roll over onto knees. The Center lifts and you come up. Stomp with the left foot. Step to the side with the right foot. Bring the left foot to it. Make a half-turn with the right foot and sling the arms up. Repeat, step, step. Then to the other side. (Use waltz music.)

Lesson Plan Fourteen

ONE: Work with the Jacob's Ladder stretch until you feel loose.

TWO: Shred hands from wrists, forearms from elbows, arms from shoulders, arms and shoulders from Center. Shred feet from ankles, lower legs from knees, legs from hip, legs from Center.

THREE: One foot in front of the other, think of being pushed in hard at the navel, so that you fall into the lower back, expanding it. Step forward with the back foot, coming down with emphasis. Swing the other leg up to the front and let it fall to the back as you continue to fall back in big steps. This can be varied by a big step forward and tiny steps falling back.

THREE

FOUR: Swing a long leg out forward and up, stretching out through the big toe. Swing arms in opposition. Energize the swing forward and let all energy leak away on the fall down. Then swing the leg as far to the back as to the front. Work from Center. The top of the head moves toward the big toe of the swinging leg. Advance to swinging the leg forward, back, forward and then step, two, three. Stretch through the big toe to the front and to the back. Alternate legs. This will lead into leaps.

FIVE: After the leg swings forward and back a few times, do it walking slowly. This movement starts at the top of the head and the legs reflect the head's forward motion. The leg swings forward, back and forward. Step, two, three, and on three the other leg swings, following the movement of the head. Accent the swing to the back, drawing the leg up.

FIVE

SIX: Partners face each other, holding each other's wrists. Stand with right foot forward. Slowly sit down, coming to rest on your left foot. Let go of each other's hands. Draw in the abdomen and think up through the head, as high as possible. Put your weight on the left leg to get up without your hands to help. Or, roll back and rest on your back, completely relaxed. Then roll forward quickly with one knee bent. Put your weight on that foot and come up. Go up and down a number of times.

SEVEN: SICKLE MOON. Stand with legs apart. Swing arms up to one side, shoulder height, and then down and up to the other side, back down and around up over the head, down around to the other side. Half-circle, half-circle, circle and a half. As you swing over the head, make a complete turn. Think up very high. (Waltz music suggested.)

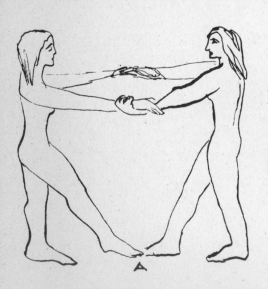

SIX

Lesson Plan Fifteen

ONE: Start with a parallel arm stretch. Move on it. Rest by allowing the head and arms to come over from the back Center. Let the knees give. Move the head and arms toward the back, then raise them in a stretch. Rest and stretch several times. Repeat.

TWO: With one foot in front of the other, fall forward and step, two, three. In other words, let your torso fall forward as you take three large steps. This will throw the Center over the front knee. Press down on the front foot and it will send a line of energy up from the floor into the body and up through the head, bringing the body up through. The back foot comes forward and you repeat—fall, step, two, three.

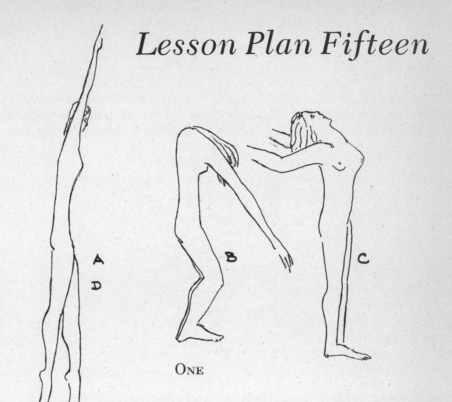

ONE

TWO

THREE: On one of the falls go down to the floor with the forward leg folded under you. Keep the other leg straight and long out to the back. Bend forward, two, three, with the chest close to the front knee. Then move the chest on to the floor in front of the knee and stretch the back leg up high. Raise the head up from the Center. Repeat on the other side.

THREE

FOUR: Lie on one side, curl in tightly with your head to your knees and your arms around the knees. On an impulse, straighten out and lie flat on your back with legs, head and arms stretched out in five points. Then roll over onto the other side and repeat a number of times, first one side, then the other.

FIVE: Sit with one leg out long to one side and the other leg folded and slightly to the front. Keep the abdomen in and pull up very tall, no folds at the waist. Extend the arms out to the side of the long leg on a plane with your shoulders. Think out through the fingertips. Push the waist out to the side of folded leg. Relax arms and head down and then move them around and up so that the head is pulled up tall, while the arms stretch out through the fingertips to the side of the extended leg and the waist pulls over to the other side. Repeat six times. To change sides, draw in at the navel and reverse leg positions. Repeat six times to the other side. Then alternate sides. Concentrate on keeping the abdomen in.

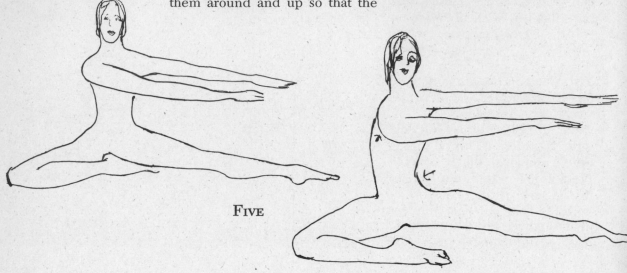

FIVE

SIX: Lie on your side with the folded leg underneath. Stretch the bottom arm out long with the palm turned up. The top arm is folded, the hand resting on the floor for balance. Swing the long top leg forward and far back. Hold it there. Change positions to the other side, rolling over backward.

SEVEN: ICE SKATING TO WALTZ MUSIC. Standing, start with feet together and slide one leg out at a diagonal. The other leg lifts off the floor. Turn the sliding foot in, out, in, out as it moves on the diagonal. The other foot comes up to meet it and takes the movement, as you lift the foot that you were just using. Imagine an ice skater in motion and the sequence of movements will be easy to understand.

SIX

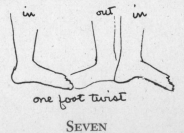

one foot twist

SEVEN

Lesson Plan Sixteen

ONE: Start with the Jacob's Ladder stretch, working until you feel loosened.

TWO: Lift the head and arms up from the Center and move them over out to one side. Then raise them up and over to the other side. Move from side to side a number of times. With arms out to one side, think out through the fingertips and top of the head. The opposite leg will lift and fall toward that side. Allow the movement to continue for two or three steps. Think further out through the fingertips and the top of the head, then raise them up and over a high arc to the other side. Continue from side to side. When tired, relax arms when the body moves, come up through and then lift the head and arms on a fresh impulse.

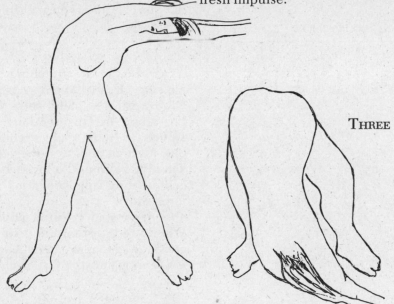

THREE: Start with feet together and arms up above your head. Arms and head move out to one side in an arc. The opposite leg moves out to its side as you swing the torso, head and arms down, around and up. The arms come to shoulder height. Then the torso swings back down, around and up, with the arms coming over the head. As the arms pass over the head bring the feet together. Opposite leg moves out to the side as arms start down to the other side. The knees always give on the swing down. Repeat.

THREE

FOUR: On the floor, do Exercise Five of Lesson Plan Fifteen.

FIVE: Sit with one leg folded and one leg out long to the side. Start facing front and make a quarter-turn. Return to the front, then turn to the other side. Do this fairly fast, about four turns to each side. Then move in a full circle, a quarter-turn at a time, pivoting on the buttocks. Feel the up-through at each turn. Tuck in tighter and tighter at the abdominal center. Repeat to the other side, a number of times. Rest, then roll together and up onto your feet.

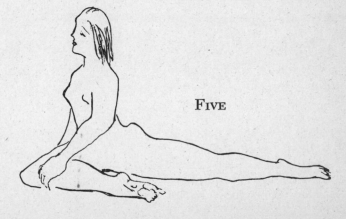

FIVE

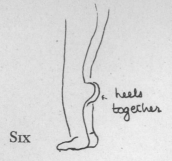

SIX

SIX: Concentrate on your heels. They are together as if they were stuck. Come up, up, up and then down. Continue raising the heels and bringing them down for some time. Add a jump, always coming down curled in, knees relaxed and heels softly down. Then jump on quarter-turns. Really get the heels up and the feet ex-tended down. Feel the energy in your feet. Next you can raise and lower alternate heels, as sparkles on water.

Let the feet waltz and the arms move side to side—half-circle, half-circle, then a whole circle over the head and then another half-circle.

Lesson Plan Seventeen

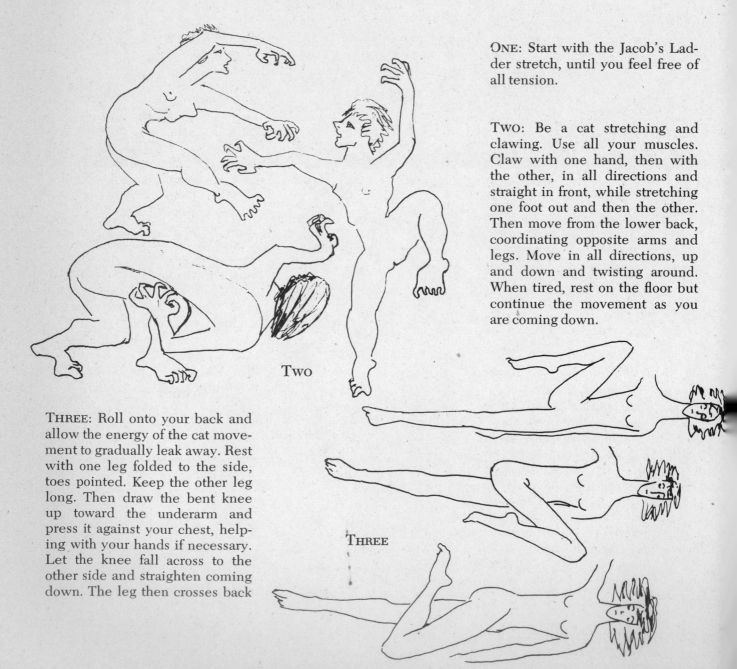

ONE: Start with the Jacob's Ladder stretch, until you feel free of all tension.

TWO: Be a cat stretching and clawing. Use all your muscles. Claw with one hand, then with the other, in all directions and straight in front, while stretching one foot out and then the other. Then move from the lower back, coordinating opposite arms and legs. Move in all directions, up and down and twisting around. When tired, rest on the floor but continue the movement as you are coming down.

TWO

THREE

THREE: Roll onto your back and allow the energy of the cat movement to gradually leak away. Rest with one leg folded to the side, toes pointed. Keep the other leg long. Then draw the bent knee up toward the underarm and press it against your chest, helping with your hands if necessary. Let the knee fall across to the other side and straighten coming down. The leg then crosses back to its own side. Come back to starting position and rest the leg before repeating. Allow it to relax until the inner part of the thigh feels as if it wants to draw up. Repeat the movement with the same leg several times. Then change legs and work on the opposite side. Then work both legs together. Hold both knees against the chest, and allow them to fall out heavily, each to its own side. Legs straighten, pull down, come together and fold at the knees to draw up again to the chest. Repeat. Use slow, relaxing music.

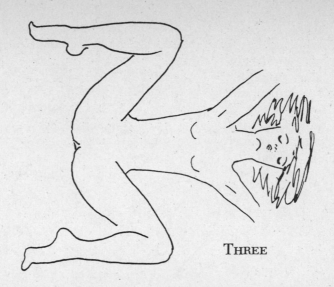

THREE

FOUR

FOUR: Still lying on your back draw knees and head together, pushing your waist to the floor. Stretch out, keeping waist down. Repeat.

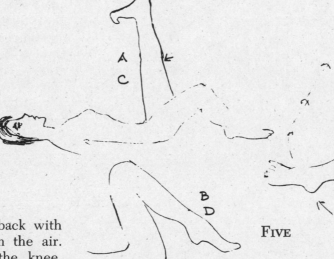

FIVE

FIVE: Relax on your back with one leg straight up in the air. Stretch the back of the knee. Push the heel up and the toes down to flex the raised foot. Drop the leg from the knee and allow it to bounce. Stretch the leg up and flex the foot again. Drop the lower part again and circle it around from the knee. Repeat a number of times. Then raise the other leg and repeat the same action several times. Finally, raise both legs and move them together.

SIX: With one leg up in the air, stretch the heel up, relax, stretch, relax. Feel all the muscles in your leg. Then circle the foot from the ankle. Change leg positions and repeat with the other foot. Then both together.

SIX

SEVEN: Still on your back, spread your legs comfortably with the knees bent and up. Bounce the knees outward. Then straighten the legs, keeping the spread, and raise them off the floor. Move them in circles from the hips, maintaining the diagonal stretch and keeping the legs straight.

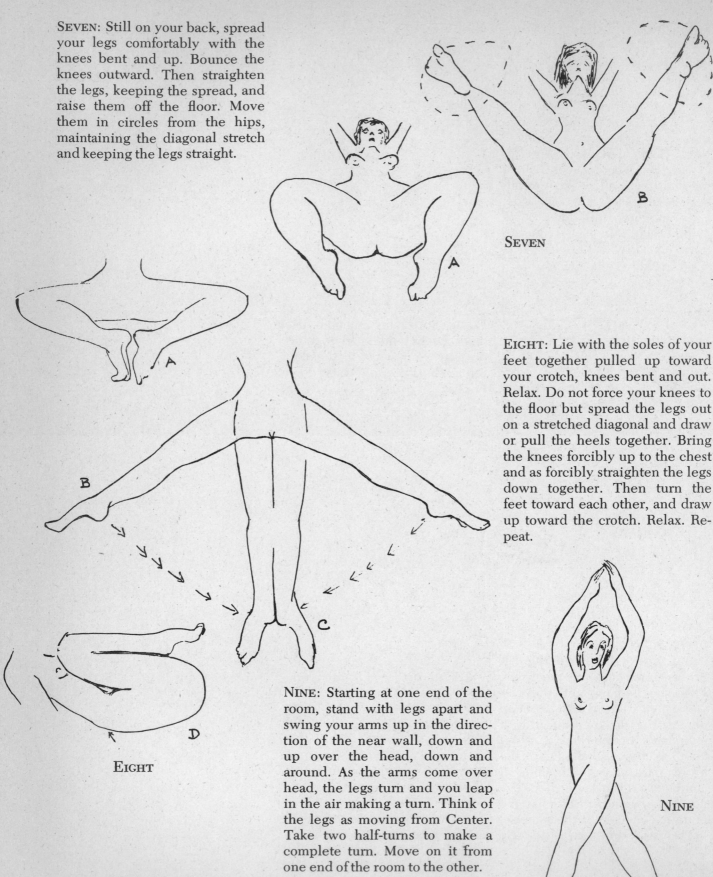

SEVEN

EIGHT: Lie with the soles of your feet together pulled up toward your crotch, knees bent and out. Relax. Do not force your knees to the floor but spread the legs out on a stretched diagonal and draw or pull the heels together. Bring the knees forcibly up to the chest and as forcibly straighten the legs down together. Then turn the feet toward each other, and draw up toward the crotch. Relax. Repeat.

EIGHT

NINE: Starting at one end of the room, stand with legs apart and swing your arms up in the direction of the near wall, down and up over the head, down and around. As the arms come over head, the legs turn and you leap in the air making a turn. Think of the legs as moving from Center. Take two half-turns to make a complete turn. Move on it from one end of the room to the other.

NINE

Lesson Plan Eighteen

ONE: Start with the Jacob's Ladder stretch to relax the body.

TWO: Stand up tall with legs apart. Extend one arm out to the side at shoulder level (A). Tuck in and half-sit low. The raised arm moves across the body to the other side (B). Come up through as the leg on the side of the raised arm also comes across the body (C). Move the arm back and stretch it up on its own side, as the other arm comes across the body. At the same time, the foot drops to the floor on its opposite side (D). The arms and leg come back to their original positions (E). Resume the half-sit, keeping tucked-in, and cross both arms in front of you (F). Then stretch up as the body comes up through (G). Continue for a while.

THREE: When you feel the rhythm well-established in your body, stress the up-through and feel the energy come out through the arms. Swing both arms to one side at shoulder level, at the same time swinging the leg on that side straight up and out to the other side, toes pointed. Hold the position and lift the heel of the standing leg. Stamp it down emphatically. Let the raised leg come down to the floor, remaining in a crossed-over position. Shift your weight onto the front foot and bring the other leg out to its own side and then swing it up and across the other leg as the arms come down and up. The arms and free leg move in opposite directions. Repeat, then move across the room. The stamp of the heel should send the arms away from the direction in which you are going, as if waving farewell. Linger at hip with leg stretched out. Stamp heel, then up on toes. Continue the length of the room. Repeat to the other side of the room.

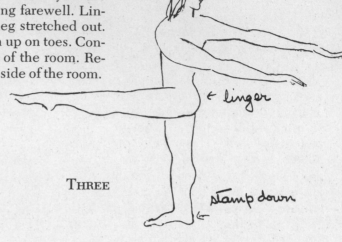

THREE

A B C

FOUR: With your legs wide apart and feet turned out, rise up on your toes and extend your arms out diagonally. (A) Make a quarter-turn to one side. (B) Push out through the front knee as the back knee descends to the floor. (C) Come straight up onto the toes and pivot a quarter-turn to the front. Repeat to the other side. Turn to both sides a number of times.

FOUR

FIVE: One foot in front of the other, sit on the back heel, come up, pivot, and sit to the other side. Repeat a number of times and end in the seated position.

FIVE

SIX: Sit on the floor with one leg extended out to the side. Fold the other leg in. Contract the abdomen, tuck in and come up on the folded knee. Push through at the crotch and turn the lower part of the folded leg to the back. Bend the knee of the extended leg, put your weight on that foot, and fold the body so that the Center is over that knee. Then come up and rise to standing, straight and stretched, and change the back foot to the front. Kneel again, moving the Center out over the front knee and dropping the torso and head forward. As you continue

down, center the body between your legs as the knees turn, suck in at the navel and come back to the original position of sitting with one knee folded and the other leg extended to the side.

A variation of this is to start from a standing position, one leg in a long step in front of the other. (A) The arms come up and the Center moves over the front foot. The back leg swings forward, back and then forward again, coming down to rest as the front leg. The front knee bends, the back leg is long. (B) The Center sinks down past the front knee

to the floor and up. The weight over the front knee and the pressure down through the front foot cause an up-through. The Center is extended forward as you rise. Do this a number of times between repetitions of the last pattern.

SEVEN: Standing, walk slowly with arms down, feet flat on the floor and body buoyed up by a high chest wall. Think of breathing in the fragrance of a favorite flower.

Lesson Plan Nineteen

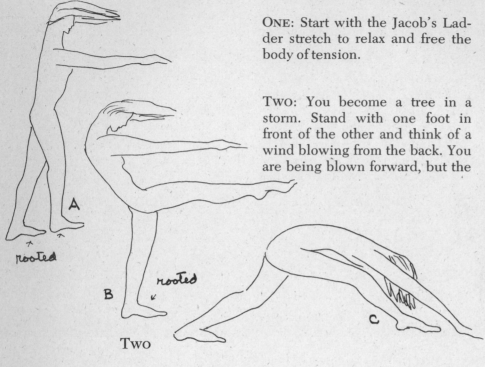

A

rooted

B

rooted

Two

C

ONE: Start with the Jacob's Ladder stretch to relax and free the body of tension.

TWO: You become a tree in a storm. Stand with one foot in front of the other and think of a wind blowing from the back. You are being blown forward, but the feet (roots) resist. The Center resists. The wind can pick up the front leg and the arms, but the back foot stays rooted fast. (B) Swing the free leg down far forward and fall heavily over the front knee. Come back to the original position. (A) Do this about six times with the same leg before changing to the other. Then the Center moves across and over the bent front knee. Press down on front foot and feel a line of energy come up through. When you are stretched highest, the back leg moves forward, the knee bends, and the Center comes forward over the bent knee as before. Repeat for a while.

THREE: Stand with legs apart, torso hanging forward from the end of the spine. Move from side to side through the hips and the knees. Let your arms move with the torso. Bend the knee on the side that you are moving toward, but keep the other knee straight. Rise a little on each swing, and keep coming up until you are straight up and allow your head to hang over backward from the Center. (D) Continuing to move from side to side, come back down. Repeat up and down about six times. This can be done with a group forming a circle and holding hands.

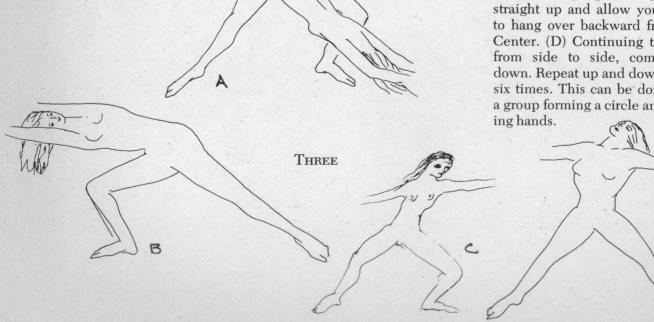

A

B

THREE

C

D

FOUR: With legs together and arms over your head in a high stretch, turn completely through the hips and spread your legs as your torso comes down, hanging over from the hips. Move up and down about six times. Twist the hips first to one side and then to the other each time you come down.

FIVE: Start as low as possible, legs spread, and turn as you come up. Lower the torso and repeat about six times. Then stretch up as high as possible and collapse to the floor. Rest. Think of breathing in the fragrance of pine as you lie under pine trees.

SIX: Stretch out on the floor. Think of a starfish. Extend all five points, head, fingertips and toes. Bring one leg up and fold it to the chest, then the other leg. Move one arm up and let it settle around the leg. Let the other arm do the same. Raise the head up and over toward the knees. Each point comes apart separately and then all stretch at the same time. Then, one by one, they slowly come together.

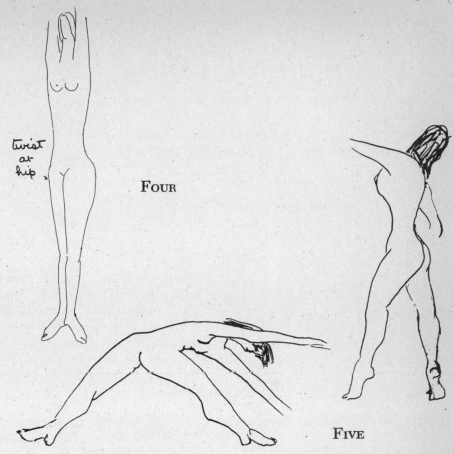

twist at hip

FOUR

FIVE

SEVEN: Slowly roll to one side. Roll over onto your back and to the other side, ironing out the back. Rest on each side, balancing on hip and shoulder.

EIGHT: Sit up, legs straight out in front, and concentrate on canoeing. Scoot one hip and leg forward together, then the other hip and leg. The arms come around toward the back on the side that is moving. The head faces that side. Canoe the length of the room, first forward, then backward. As you move backward, pull in at the waist and expand the lower back.

NINE: Fold both knees to one side, shift your weight onto your knees, bring one foot forward flat on the floor, and come up in stages with your weight over the front knee. Press down through the front foot and come up partially. Move the back leg forward and bring the body weight over that knee. Each time come higher until you are finally standing tall.

TEN: Work at figure eights across the room, both arms coming up to one side overhead, then straight down the middle and up the other side, over the head and straight down the middle again. Move freely, but keep the form.

Lesson Plan Twenty

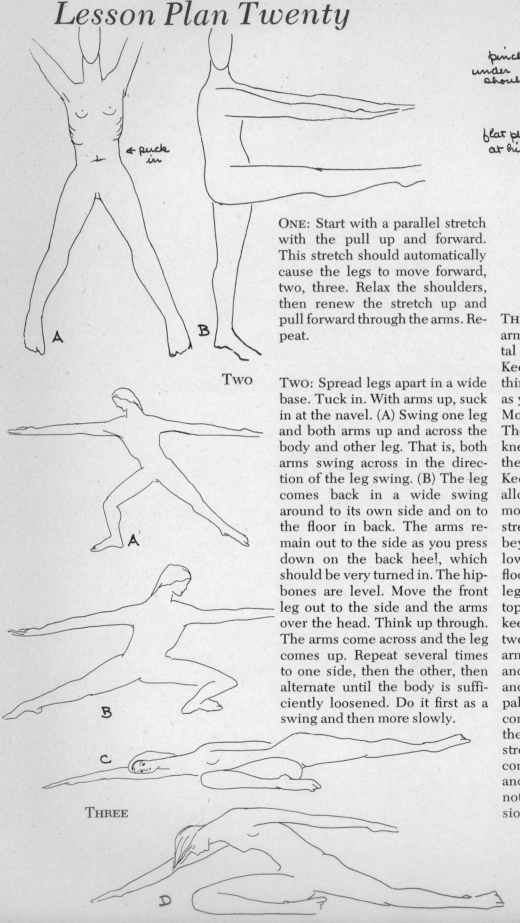

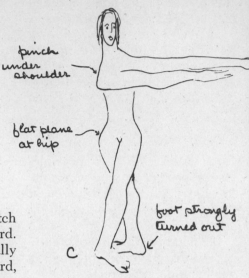

pinch under shoulder

flat plane at hip

foot strongly turned out

← puck in

Two

A

B

C

THREE

D

ONE: Start with a parallel stretch with the pull up and forward. This stretch should automatically cause the legs to move forward, two, three. Relax the shoulders, then renew the stretch up and pull forward through the arms. Repeat.

TWO: Spread legs apart in a wide base. Tuck in. With arms up, suck in at the navel. (A) Swing one leg and both arms up and across the body and other leg. That is, both arms swing across in the direction of the leg swing. (B) The leg comes back in a wide swing around to its own side and on to the floor in back. The arms remain out to the side as you press down on the back heel, which should be very turned in. The hipbones are level. Move the front leg out to the side and the arms over the head. Think up through. The arms come across and the leg comes up. Repeat several times to one side, then the other, then alternate until the body is sufficiently loosened. Do it first as a swing and then more slowly.

THREE: Stand with a wide base, arms out to the sides on a horizontal plane with the shoulders. Keep the feet well grounded and think out through the fingertips as you move from side to side. (A) Move the chest from side to side. The underarms move past the knees, which bend slightly with the movement. Do several times. Keep it high for a while, then allow the knees to bend more and more. (B) The arms continue to stretch out from side to side, beyond the knees, and you go lower and lower. Stretch onto the floor on your side with the folded leg down and the bottom arm and top leg extended. (C) Feel and keep the stretched tension between the fingers of the bottom arm and the toes of the top leg, and between the end of the spine and the top of the head. Keep palms down. Retain tension and come up, raising the back Center, then getting up on the knee and stretching out through the arms, coming up higher and higher. Up and down a number of times. Do not relax on the floor or the tension will be lost.

FOUR: Down on the floor, roll onto your back and rest peacefully.

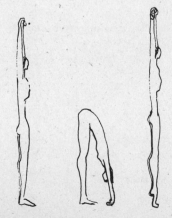

FIVE: Picture the ocean and a calm before a storm. Whitecaps appear. One arm shoots or quivers upward and relaxes back. The other arm, a leg, the other leg, the head, separately dart up a few times, and then relax back. The ocean becomes wild, with big peaked waves. The arms, legs and head shoot up together and fall back. Continue for some time. The waves roll on. Head, arms and legs rise up and roll you over to one side. All extensions draw in, then shoot out, up and over to the other side. Continue this for some time.

SIX

SEVEN: Think of a seagull. Stand high on your toes, right foot forward. Stretch arms out at a diagonal, one up, the other down. Think of them as the wide-spread wings of a seagull. Stretch from fingertips to fingertips. Pull up through the higher arm, pull, two, three. Pull down through lower arm, two, three. Then the arms change positions. This will develop into large, wheeling turns.

SIX: Roll over onto one knee. Draw up the back Center. Think of the Center as the peak of a wave. It comes up and falls down, comes up and falls down. The movement is quite free and you rise and fall with it. One knee or the other comes up. The wave reaches its crest and you come up and up, high. Fall down and over to the floor, roll and come up again. End quietly on the floor, feeling the waves of energy subside, then quietly roll up onto the other knee and come up again as before.

SEVEN

Lesson Plan Twenty-One

ONE: A Sapling Tree stretch. Think of reaching for a branch of a sapling tree. Grasp it and pull down violently. Allow yourself to spring up just as violently on a terrific stretch.

TWO: Feel you are a comet. Feet together, tuck in and half-sit with arms relaxed. Pull up and up with an inner stretch up through the head. Come up on your toes as you stretch. Renew the tuck-in and come down on your heels as you half-sit again. Repeat for some time. Then, on the up-through, shoot one leg and both arms out to the side. Turn your head toward the extended leg and hop the opposite way on the standing leg. Let the arms and extended leg drop. Repeat until you have gone the length of the room, then come back, with legs reversed. Do this at least twice in each direction, imagining that the extended leg is the tail of a comet.

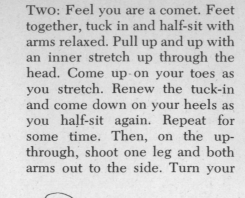

Two

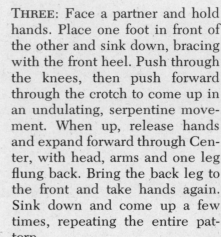

hop in this direction →

THREE: Face a partner and hold hands. Place one foot in front of the other and sink down, bracing with the front heel. Push through the knees, then push forward through the crotch to come up in an undulating, serpentine movement. When up, release hands and expand forward through Center, with head, arms and one leg flung back. Bring the back leg to the front and take hands again. Sink down and come up a few times, repeating the entire pattern.

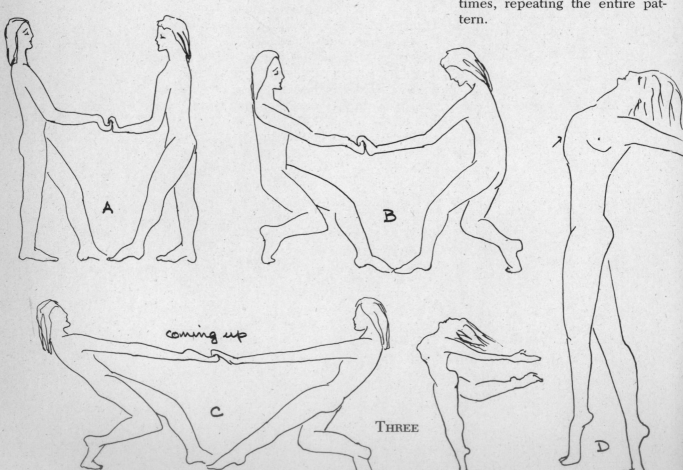

coming up

A

B

C

THREE

D

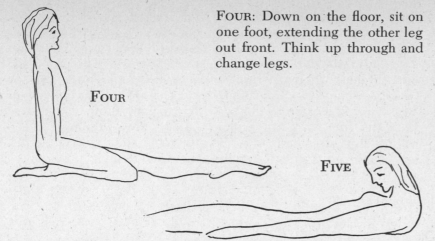

FOUR

FIVE

FOUR: Down on the floor, sit on one foot, extending the other leg out front. Think up through and change legs.

FIVE: Rest on the floor, letting the spine go as if it were a slack rope. The tail clicks under and a line of energy goes up through the head. The head and shoulders roll up. Press the vertebrae down to the floor, one by one, from the back Center to the head. Repeat three times and on the fourth time up move the head in a large, very slow circle, to one side and then around to the other side. Circle the head three times each way.

SIX: Use gentle music for the head movement (e.g., Sibelius' "Valse Triste"). Continue to move to this music as you roll over to one side and rise up and down and up a few times.

SEVEN: Come up onto your feet and move freely to the music.

Lesson Plan Twenty-Two

This is a good lesson for winter months.

ONE: Think of bare trees etched against the sky. Stretch with legs apart and arms up on a diagonal. Think of strong winds blowing the branches (arms) all around, in all directions. Let the torso go with it, but keep the feet rooted. The wind lets up. The arms shred out quietly, one movement blending into the next, until finally the arms drop slowly.

ONE

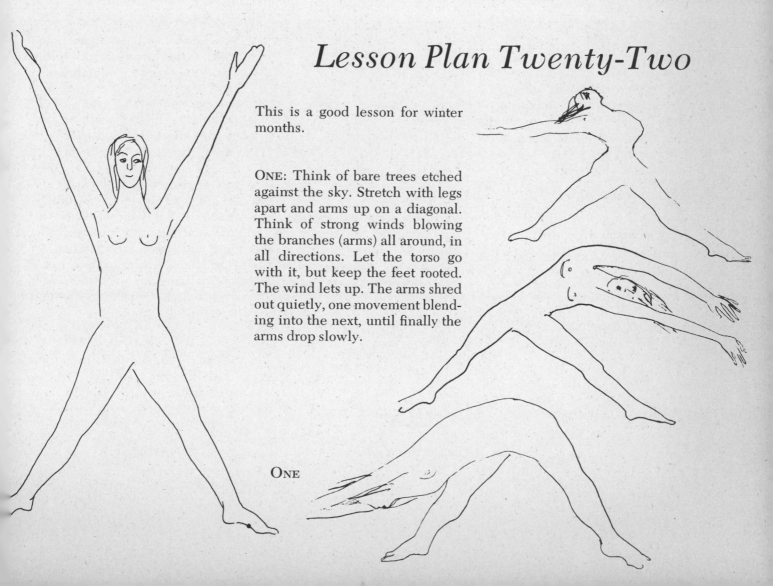

TWO: Feet together, both arms stretched out to one side. Think of pulling a boat in to shore by a rope. Pull through the underarm, then through the lower back as the arms come down and slightly across, losing tension as they do. Bring the arms back to the original position, stretched out to the side. As the arms stretch out, the leg on the opposite side moves out from the hip to its side. As the arms come down, the other leg is drawn up to it. The pull is to the side, the underarm, waist, lower back and hip all drawing the arms down and across. Do this very slowly. Move to one side across the room, then reverse the movement and return.

Two

THREE: With strong tuck-in, legs wide apart and knees bent, come up on the toes and down on the heel of one foot. Repeat on the other foot. Alternate a few times, then up on the toes and down on the heels of both feet.

FOUR: Sit backward onto the floor with legs still wide apart.

FIVE: Lie with legs spread, arms out horizontal. Swing one leg across, up, around and down. Then swing the other. Do this continuously to fast-paced music.

SIX: Draw the legs together and wait for the lower back to settle. Turn over onto your stomach. Look down, open the eyes and look up. Allow the eyes to rest. Do this six times. Look from side to side six times. Roll eyes in a circle, six times clockwise and six times counterclockwise. Open the eyes very wide, look up and let the head movement follow the eyes. Stretch your back as you look, raising one vertebra at a time until you are standing on your knees. Bring one foot up flat on the floor and move the Center over that knee. Come up onto your feet.

SEVEN: Walk gently, being aware of life through your eyes as if you were in the woods and there was so much to see all around. Follow the movement of your eyes.

Five

Lesson Plan Twenty-Three

ONE: Start with the Jacob's Ladder stretch.

TWO: Place one foot in front of the other and stand tall. Raise the back leg up as high as possible toward the back, with the knee straight. Keeping the leg at that same high level, with straight knee, move the leg slowly out and around to the front. Bring it down so it takes the place of the front foot. If you do this quickly, it will make for a small jump. The other leg now lifts to the back and comes around. Repeat for a while. Then reverse the movement, moving the front leg up and around to the back. Move the opposite arm in the same direction as the leg.

Two

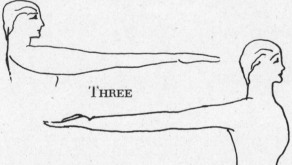

THREE

THREE: Extend one arm out long to the front at shoulder height. Let it come down and up to the back, stretched, and then bring it down and back to the front. Do this for some time with one arm, then with the other.

FOUR: Be a water wheel. Move one shoulder up, to the front, down, to the back and around in as large a circle as possible. Think of the shoulder as a wheel, the arm as water, dripping. Reverse the direction; then circle with the other shoulder. Then move both shoulders together, this time imagining waves rolling in.

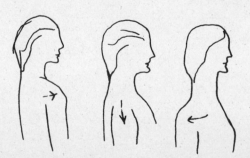

FOUR

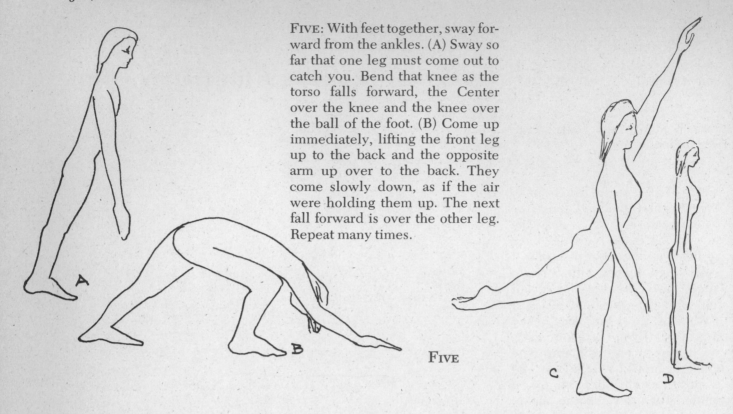

FIVE: With feet together, sway forward from the ankles. (A) Sway so far that one leg must come out to catch you. Bend that knee as the torso falls forward, the Center over the knee and the knee over the ball of the foot. (B) Come up immediately, lifting the front leg up to the back and the opposite arm up over to the back. They come slowly down, as if the air were holding them up. The next fall forward is over the other leg. Repeat many times.

FIVE

SIX: Allow the front knee to give completely, so that the back leg trails out on the floor. Relax face down with your forehead on the floor. Then folded leg straightens out to the back. With arms in front of you and bent at the elbows so that your weight is on the fore- arms, imagine being a seal on the beach. Lift the back Center, drawing in first your right flipper (arm) and then your left until you are raised up with your arms fairly straight. Slowly lift your head and blink your eyes, as if you were focusing on clouds at the horizon. Watch them move up straight overhead. Then stretch back in an over-arc as far as you can go. Do this four times. The torso should be resting on the hip- bones. Move your arms down again until your forearms are on the floor.

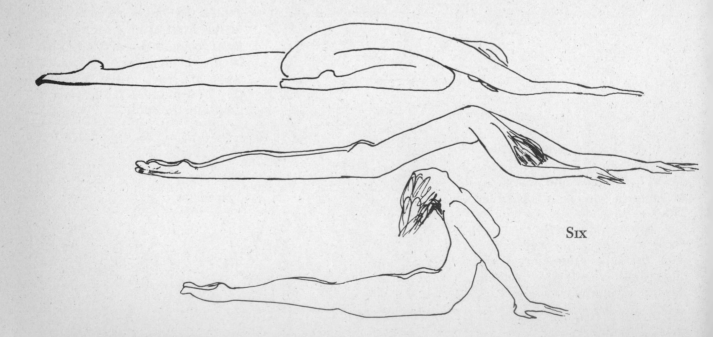

SIX

SEVEN: Turn your head to one side and follow the movement of the clouds up and around to the other side. The head will make a broad, soft circle from the throat. Rest your eyes and allow your arms to come down completely to the floor. Relax completely. Come back up on your forearms and circle your head from the other side. When you bring the arms forward or back, be sure the movement comes from the shoulders. The arms are soft. The movement to rise comes from the back Center. Lift the whole torso from the Center and come back to sit on your heels with the body relaxed forward. Lift further at the center and bring one knee up, raise the center over the knee and stand. (Waltz music suggested.)

EIGHT

NINE

EIGHT: SOFT MIST. Arms and legs move in opposition. Arms go around body to one side as the leg moves across in the opposite direction. Step, two, three, reversing positions of arms as the other leg crosses over.

NINE: Arms swing up to the right and down and then up to the left like the letter U. They come up high on both sides. Feel the down movement in the abdomen and tuck in. On the third time up step out to that side, and as you come down let that knee bend. Bring the feet together on the next swing up. Continue for some time.

Lesson Plan Twenty-Four

ONE: Stretch as if pulling on a sapling tree as in Lesson Plan Twenty-One, Exercise One. Pull down and up violently.

TWO: THE MAYPOLE. Feet together, tuck in, keep knees slightly bent. Think of the arms as hanging down from Center, very long. Wrap them around the body to one side. Lift the Center high and let the arms swing and wrap themselves around the body the other way. Do this

TWO

slowly at first and then quickly. Keep the feet together in place.

THREE: Think of a top spinning across the floor. The arms swing around at shoulder height turning the body rapidly.

FOUR: Stand with one foot in front of the other, with the heel of the back foot slightly raised and its big toe touching heel of front foot. Let the arms hang relaxed at the sides and the Center relax down. Tuck in. Press down on the front foot and feel the line of energy come up through. On the up-through, the big toe of the back foot draws a circle around to the front and ends with its heel touching the big toe of the other foot. The Center goes down and the weight is on both feet. Let the back heel come up in preparation for drawing a circle. The weight now shifts onto the front foot and the other foot circles around. Bring the arms up in front in a rounded position. Feel a mental connection between the finger-

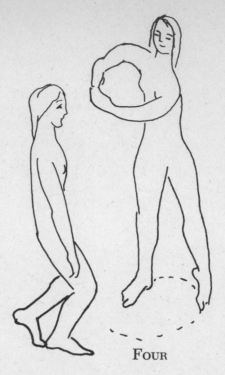

FOUR

tips. Move the arms in opposition to the legs, around to the back until you feel a pinch at the back Center. Release and let the arms move around to the other side.

FIVE: Feel the mist rolling in. Stand with feet apart, one arm pulled straight up. Bring it over an arc, over the head and down the other side to the floor. Your weight should shift to the leg on the side of the downward movement. Release the other leg and let it move across in front of the weight-bearing leg. Transfer the weight to the front foot and let the back leg move out straight to the side. The arm sweeps across the floor to its own side. Come up. Repeat, moving the whole length of the room, then reverse and come back again.

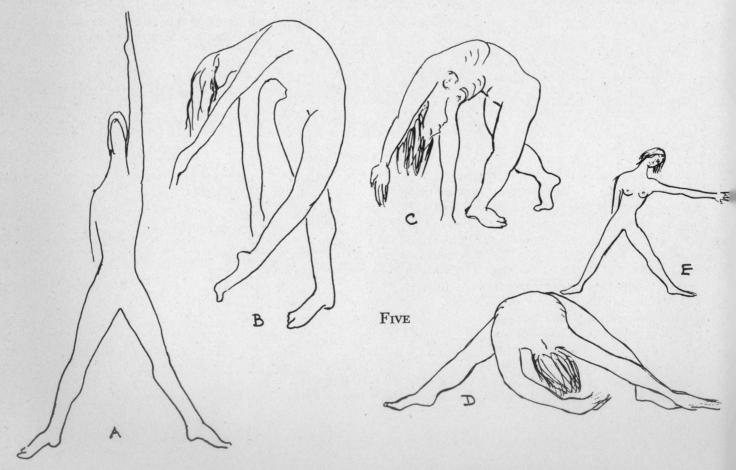

A   B   FIVE   C   D   E

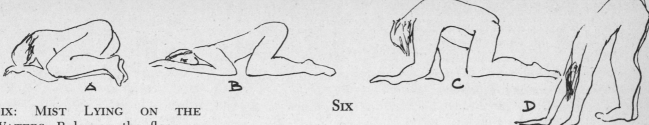

SIX

SIX: MIST LYING ON THE WATERS. Relax on the floor on your side. Think of mist settling down on water. The body draws together, with knees and head in toward the Center. The sides of the ribs should feel soft and flexible. The mist rises; the body rolls over onto the knees and slowly unfolds up. The mist is gone. Think of waking up in the woods observed by woodland creatures. Feel very alive and aware. The lower back softly rounds, and one leg stretches out through the big toe. Stretch and land on that foot. Stretch through the other big toe and land on that foot.

SEVEN: Stretch through one big toe, step on that foot, stretch through the other big toe and jump with feet together. Reach, step, reach and jump. Then feel as if the lower back is breathing up and release one foot up, then the other. Gather internal force and jump together. Stretch and yawn, breathing in the fragrance of the air, and leave the room on tiptoe.

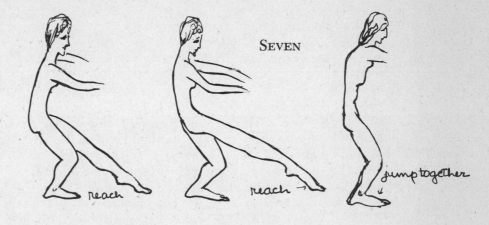

SEVEN

reach

reach →

jump together

Lesson Plan Twenty-Five

ONE: Imagine it is sunrise and you are out for a brisk early morning walk. Progress from walking to striding, running, leaping and then ease back into a brisk walk. Feel alive and tall, springing off each foot as it touches the ground.

TWO: With feet together, stand up tall and look straight forward. Turn the right foot out, come up on toes, heels close together. Circle in one spot by bringing the turned out left foot up on toes, up toe, up toe, to the right foot. (Up toe, up toe means that the foot is on its toes and then lifted off the floor and returned.) Turn the right foot out on the toes and bring the left foot to it on the toes. Come down on the right heel, then up. Turn continuously in one direction for a long time. Then change directions. Come down on the right heel for right turns and the left heel for left turns. The pressure is down on the heel. Come up through on the turns three times. The turns become fast, then slow. The arms rise and fall. You become a whirling dervish.

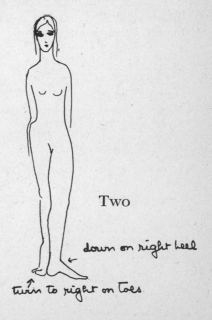

TWO

← down on right heel

turn to right on toes

THREE: POPPY IN A HOT SUN. The head lets go at the base of the neck. The chin draws in. Breathe up from wherever the head rests. Let the head go. Rest. Breathe up. While the head is down, feel as if there are weights in the head, causing it to hang heavily. Feel them roll as you circle it around. After breathing up again, drop over from the shoulders and circle around from there. Stay with the head and shoulders for some time. Then relax over from the Center, the waist, the hips, and then relax the knees and ankles. The head and each part of the body moves around in a circle, then hangs and rests. Then you breathe up and drop over to the next unit, lower and lower until you are down on the floor.

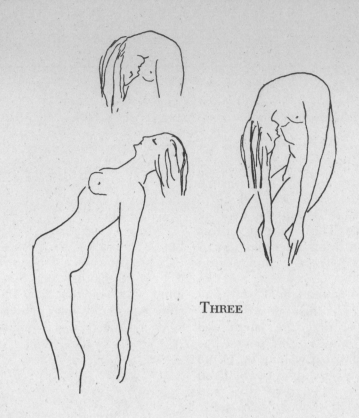

THREE

FOUR: Think of poppy seeds dropping to earth. The leaves fall and cover them. Rest quietly on the floor, the body warm and curled in on itself. The seed goes deeper under the ground, where the moisture and heat cause it to expand. The seed bursts open. The Center expands and the head, arms and legs, move out slowly, expansively and luxuriously, rolling you onto your back. Fold to the other side and expand open again onto your back.

FIVE: Lying on your back, imagine roots growing as you stretch out through the legs. Think of the legs as attached at the waist. One leg crosses over the other on a diagonal. It continues to pull until it is lying on the floor on the other side, and pulls the body over.

The head turns. You are now lying on your stomach. The other leg stretches out, up and across, scissor-wise, which causes the body to turn again onto the back. Repeat a number of times. The arms follow the movement of the body.

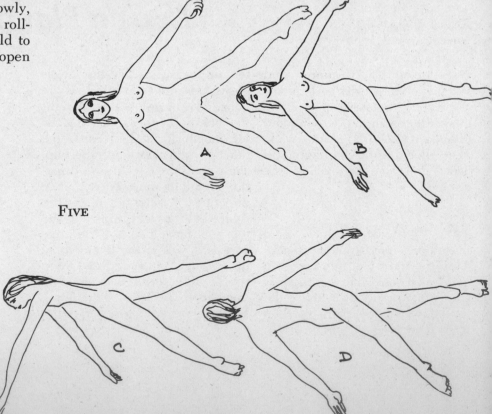

FIVE

SIX: Lie on one side, head and knees gathered together, arms around knees. Roll over onto your knees, bring one foot forward and spiral around and up to the greatest expansion, unfolding all parts of the body.

SEVEN: Bend over in a large arc to the front, head way down. Relax completely and let yourself go back down to the floor. Relax, then repeat the full cycle of spreading roots, drawing the energy together and spiraling up into the sun and air. Repeat any number of times.

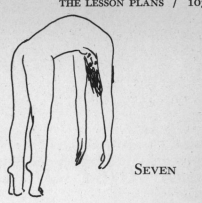

SEVEN

Lesson Plan Twenty-Six

ONE: Walking and striding as in the previous lesson.

TWO: Circle in one spot as in Lesson Twenty-Five, Exercise Two.

THREE: Imagine that it is evening and the sun is going down, throwing long shadows. You are a shadow. Stand on a wide base, one foot in front of the other, with your body at a long angle to the front. The front knee gives. The body moves forward and down as the back leg extends out behind. The body relaxes over the front knee, the back leg fully extended. The back leg then circles out and around and relaxes to the front with the knee bent. Now the other foot stretches out along the floor to the back. The toes grip the ground and the body comes up, straight out at an angle, and the back leg rises up and circles. Repeat the movement.

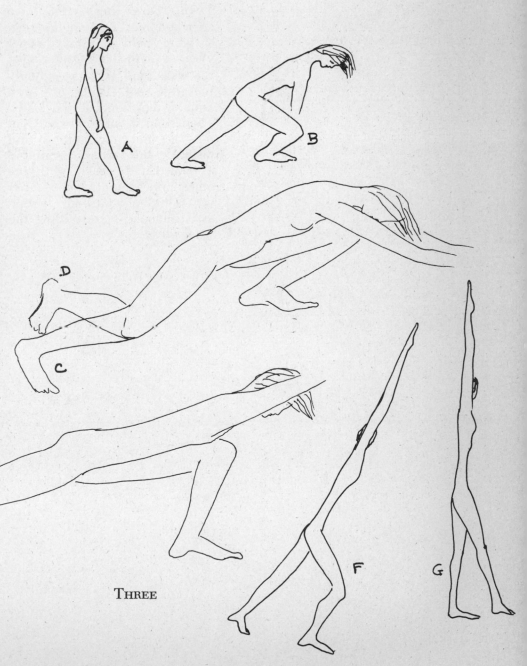

THREE

FOUR: On the floor, think of roots growing and stretch out through the legs as in Lesson Twenty-Five.

FIVE: Figure Eights to smooth, even music. (Waltz music suggested.) Description of Figure Eights on pages 40-41.

Lesson Plan Twenty-Seven

ONE: Start with the Jacob's Ladder stretch.

TWO: Tuck in, with torso stretched long. Think of the torso as being held in three distinct places: 1) at the back Center, 2) at the waist, and 3) at the strongly tucked-in tail. Bring one arm around the front of the body. Then sling it out from the Center—shoulder joint, elbow and hand. Let this take you around in a spin. Do the same with the other arm, spinning the other way. Think of your body moving as if someone were pulling the string off a top.

← in at center to back

← long waist

← strong tuck in

THREE: Pull in at the Center and tuck in. Thinking from the Center, swing one leg up out, around and down in large, energetic motions, first one leg, then the other. The force of the swing will turn the body around with the leg leading.

TWO

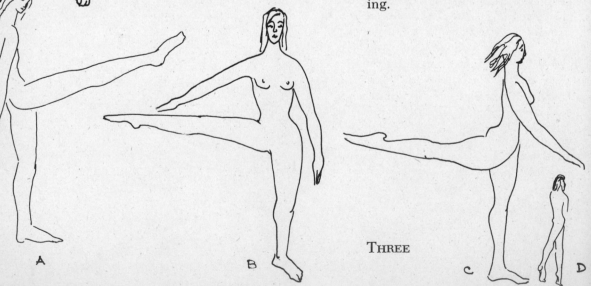

THREE

FOUR: Think of a forest breathing. Stand with legs spread and arms stretched up diagonally. Rest into the back Center and the lower back. Think of the back as being round, like a tree, and of the Center as a taproot extending down into the earth and drawing up moisture (energy). Go down in as far as possible and feel the energy well up. Think of branches spreading out wide. At the highest place up, with the arms stretched up and out turn the hands palm down and move the arms down. Move the Center down and let the knees give slightly. Repeat.

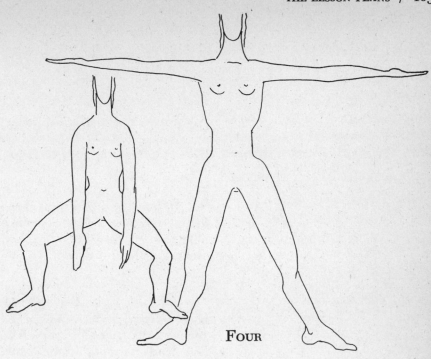

FOUR

Let the knees give even more and sit down, then lie down. Swing the legs up and back over the head in a wide spread. When the toes touch the floor, stretch out at an angle through one leg along the floor, then out through the other leg. Repeat.

FIVE: Rest on your back. Roll onto the knees and stress breathing up against the upper back Center. Come up, then down, forward onto the floor. Let the front Center touch the floor. Come up and down and up a few times.

FIVE

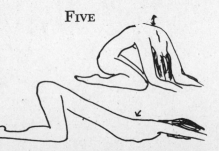

SIX: Standing, swing both arms together up and down from side to side. Swing, two, three, and the third time, swing up over the head and around. Then move on it. (Waltz music suggested.)

Lesson Plan Twenty-Eight

ONE: Start with the Jacob's Ladder stretch.

TWO: As in Lesson Twenty-Seven, think of the torso as three distinct parts and sling out alternate arms. This will spin you around in place like a top.

THREE: Swing one leg forward, back, forward and around. In the swing, think from the navel. The foot lands around to the back, crossed beyond the other foot, with a strongly turned heel. The heel pulls and you resist with the underarm on the opposite side. The leg springs back into place, next to the other. Alternate legs.

FOUR: Swing the right leg and arm out to the right side. Let the arm move up. Stamp the leg down, step, two, three to that side. Repeat to the other side. Then step, half-turn, half-turn. Repeat on alternate sides. This can be done with many music forms and rhythms.

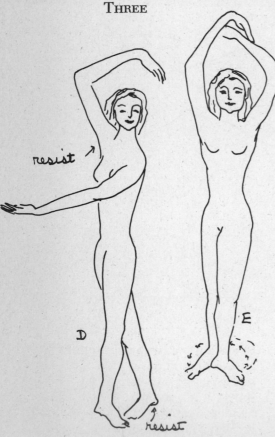

A
C
B

THREE

FOUR

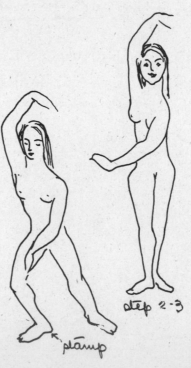

resist

D
E
resist

step 2-3

stamp

half turn - ha

step to other side

FIVE: Rest on the floor on your back. With feet on the floor and knees up, think of the hot sun and warm sand on a beach. Squidge the lower back down as if into warm sand.

SIX: Come up rolling onto the knees and stress breathing up against the upper back Center.

SEVEN: Think of a forest breathing, as in Lesson Twenty-Seven. Repeat those movements.

EIGHT: Feel your breath press up high against the Center. Walk slowly, waiting for the breath to bring you up to your toes. Return back down to your heels when the Center can no longer sustain the up breath. Continue to concentrate on the Center moving up and up. You should feel higher, and light.

Lesson Twenty-Nine

ONE: Walk as in early morning, then run, leap and back to a walk again. Feel exhilarated.

TWO: Start in a half-sitting position with feet together. Feel the up-through as the torso lifts. The legs will straighten and release one foot out to the back on the up-through. The back leg is on a slant line. As you resume the half-sitting position, it moves next to the other leg. On the next up-through the other leg is released to the back. The arms are rounded in front, fingertips almost touching. The arms move in the direction of the front foot while the head moves the opposite way. Hold the chin high, as if it were resting on a shelf. Do this in place to start.

THREE: Think of mist around mountains. Continuing with Exercise Two, move the arms at all levels. Feel the pattern in freedom then move the leg to the front on the side that the arms are moving toward. Release arms, legs, head around at the same time. Let this lead into balances and big out-and-around movements.

THREE

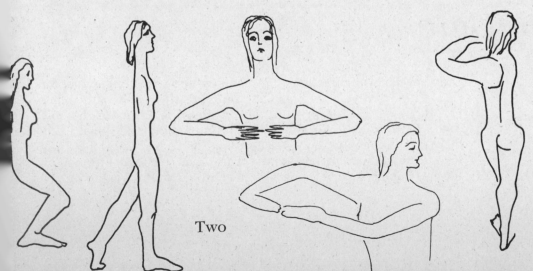

TWO

FOUR: REFLECTIONS IN WATER. With one foot in front of the other, allow the knee to bend as you move forward and down through the Center. Let the back leg slip out to the back. As the Center moves down as far as possible, feel that you see reflections in the water at your feet. The Center rises up and the body adjusts to the upright position. Rock the pelvis forward to move the back leg to the front. Walk, two, three and repeat.

FOUR

FIVE: Kneel on the floor, torso out flat. Push through at the end of the spine to bring the torso up straight, remaining on your knees. Raise your arms over your head, then lower them and your torso back down again. Next time up, stretch, raise the chest and let the head and arms move on an over-arc to the back. Repeat a number of times.

FIVE

chest high

SIX: Get up on your feet. Think creatively and move freely.

Lesson Plan Thirty

ONE: Stretch in all directions.

TWO: Tuck in and think down, then up through, in one place with feet together and toes pointing out. Repeat several times. On one up-through, slip one foot forward directly in front of the other. Lift the back leg up to the side, out and around and down to the front, replacing the other foot. The other leg then lifts up, out and around to the front to replace

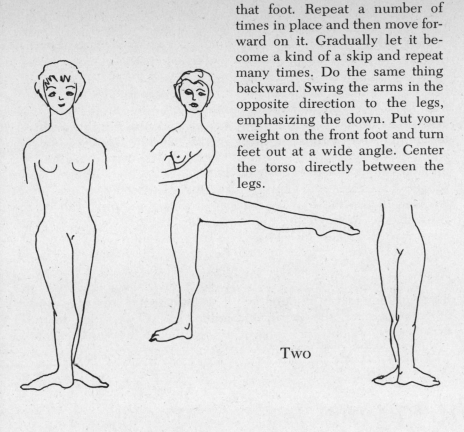

that foot. Repeat a number of times in place and then move forward on it. Gradually let it become a kind of a skip and repeat many times. Do the same thing backward. Swing the arms in the opposite direction to the legs, emphasizing the down. Put your weight on the front foot and turn feet out at a wide angle. Center the torso directly between the legs.

Two

*move forward on it
cover space*

THREE: Feel a long, trailing mist. Stand with one leg in front of the other, arms stretched out but rounded and soft at shoulder level, as if they were resting on a railing. The arms move on the breath, around to the back, toward the side of the forward leg. Turn the back foot in at a strong angle and resist with the back heel. Feel a long pull between the Center and the tucked-in tail. As the arms move as far back as possible, they unfold backward as if they were long, trailing mists, disappearing into infinity. When the pinch at back Center lets go, slowly release the back leg straight forward. The arms float softly around to the front. Then continue to the other side, the head following the direction of the arms. Keep the chest high. Feel a wave of nostalgia as the arms flow to the back.

THREE

FOUR: Walk forward, one leg directly in front of the other. Keep the chest high. Think of the breath being to the front, at the sides, the underarms and to the back. The chest is now full all around. Keep the arms softly rounded at shoulder level, and move them around toward the back on side of forward foot, eyes looking straight ahead. This is a slow, sustained and formal movement. Think up through and of smooth circles. Walk straight ahead for some time. Then, take two steps forward and on the third let the upper disk (shoulder girdle) lead into a turn to the side of the forward leg as far as possible to the back and then on around. The opposite leg resists but is slowly turned around.

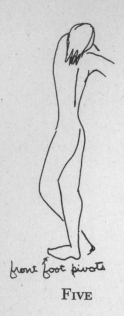

FIVE

FIVE: Continue to resist with the back leg as it slowly turns around behind. Turn the back foot out, keeping your chest high and your arms at shoulder level. Move the back leg in a circle around to the front as you pivot on the front leg. When your arms have returned to the front, take two steps forward and turn to the other side. Come up onto your toes and shift your weight to the forward foot. Move the other leg to the front as the arms change to the other side. Step, two, three and turn to the other side.

SIX: With one foot in front of the other, arms out at shoulder level over the front foot, move back through the Center. As the arms move around to the side of the front foot, adjust your weight over the back foot and come up through. Move your arms around to the other side. The front leg is released up slightly and moves to the back. Repeat the entire movement for a while. Then walk backward, step, two and turn to the back at the back underarm. Trail the rest of the body around in a slow pivot, ending with your weight on the front foot. Repeat to the other side. Step, step and turn in the direction of the back foot. On the turn, keep your weight on the whole back foot. The front foot is drawn halfway around and you continue the turn by pivoting on the new front foot.

Lesson Plan Thirty-One

ONE: Stretch up high.

TWO: One foot in front of the other, arms held out across the front foot and rounded as if holding a big beach ball, move your weight down onto the front foot and then come up on your toes as the other leg moves to the front. Your arms go down and up to the other side. Take three steps to the front. The first step is flat on your foot; the other two are on toes. On the third step turn in the direction of the back foot, with your shoulder leading. Pivot, taking three steps as you turn. First step down on the heel and then up on toes, up on toes and down on first step forward. Two more steps forward on toes and turn to the other side, keeping your arms rounded at shoulder level. On the down, arms come down.

TWO

THREE: Plumb Line. Stand with one foot in front of the other, feet turned out comfortably. The front heel and back toe should meet. Put your weight on the front foot, with the Center over the ball of the foot. Feel a plumb line drop from the Center directly down to the center of the third toe. Bring the back foot around with the heel in close to the ankle of the front foot, and drop it to the front with a heavy percussive move-

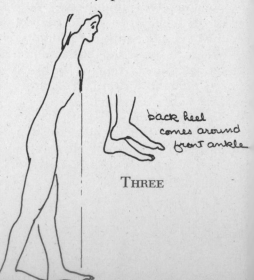

back heel comes around front ankle

THREE

ment. Do it with one foot, then the other. Repeat for a while, then allow the movement to become larger and repeat.

FOUR: As if you were on soft moss in the woods, feel free in movement. Stand with one foot in front of the other, your weight on the front foot. Sink the sole of the foot down in the soft moss and feel the coolness coming up through. Keep well tucked-in. Think of woodsy creatures and move with light, playful gestures toward the back or side or around, dodging, frolicking. (Suggested music: Mendelssohn's Overture to *A Midsummer Night's Dream*.)

FIVE: With feet comfortably apart, arms up and rounded, stand with weight on one foot and the toes of the other foot pointed out to the side. Turn your head in the direction of the point. Move your arms to the side of the

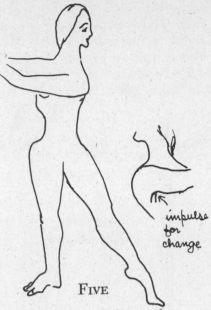

FIVE

impulse for change

weighted foot and transfer your weight to the other foot, feeling the transfer through the underarms. Pinch in somewhat at your underarm on the side of the pointed foot. Holding the body high and proud, step out to one side, cross over, step out and

point the toe and shift the weight through the underarm to the other side. Then, one, two, three, half-turn, half-turn, change. Find freedom within the restricted form.

SIX: Lying on your back, move one arm out and around from the Center in a large, extended circle. Follow the hand around with your eyes. Repeat the circle with one arm for some time. Then with the other arm. The impulse for the movement comes from the Center. Circle both arms at the same time up and around in great, extended movements crossing each other. Circle one leg in a motion that stems from the navel. Then circle the other leg, then both together. Now repeat circling all limbs at once.

SEVEN: Using waltz music, circle one leg out and around to the back, then the other leg, moving freely. Step back, two, three.

Lesson Plan Thirty-Two

ONE: JACOB'S LADDER STRETCH.

TWO: Poppy, as in Lesson Twenty-Five.

THREE: Lie on your side with your knees and head as close together as you can get them. Think of a blanket of leaves or snow covering you. The snow melts and the poppy seeds sink into the ground. The body rests down.

The sun grows hotter and the seeds begin to stir. Contract in at the Center. Relax. Repeat a number of times. Think of the seeds sprouting and stretching out rootlets in all directions. The upper body turns over onto the back, slowly, languorously. The lower body rolls after. Stretch through the head, arms and legs from the Center. Spread your legs apart as the rootlets grow in all directions. Turn over to the other side and gather in. Stretch out and gather in and repeat the stretch.

FOUR: Cross one leg over the other in a long scissors stretch. Pull the leg across until the lower torso turns over. Let the upper body follow. Repeat three or four times to one side, then to the other.

FIVE: Roll together on one side with head and knees together, contracted. Roll up onto your knees and come up in a spiral. When standing, stretch up as high as possible and collapse down to the floor. Repeat the complete cycle of the scissor stretch, the curled-up position, up-through on a spiral, the tall stretch and the collapse to the floor. Do this about six times and end standing.

SIX: WHITECAPS. Standing with heels together and arms stretched up to one side, step, two, three to that side. Move the arms down and up on the other side. Heels together and step, two, three to that side. Continue working on establishing a rhythmic pattern. (Waltz music.)

FIVE

spiral up and collapse

Lesson Plan Thirty-Three

ONE: Stretch.

TWO: Think of your body as a candle, wax melting down as a flame comes up through the wick.

THREE: Feel a fire under the earth's surface, spreading out.

Melt down to the floor and begin the movement in a round ball. As the fire spreads out under the earth, the body expands out. The fire leaps up as a volcano, and the body comes spiraling up like a flame, rising on a terrific stretch and dropping back to the earth as if lava were coming down a mountainside. Repeat the explosive cycle many times.

FOUR: A fire sweeps across the prairies. Stand on a wide base, knees bent, and think of the action as starting at the navel. Contract in. Move in and under-arc from one foot to the other. Feel the current pass from one foot to the other as you press them

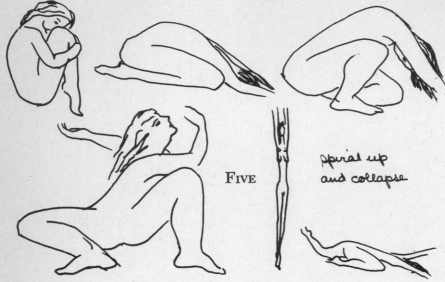

contract in at navel

pressure down

pressure down

under arc from foot to foot

FOUR

arm movement pattern

down. Let the arms gradually come into it, swinging from side to side. Build up the movement in your legs and slow down, a couple of times. The arms in the same forceful movement come up together and around. Slide one leg out to one side, bring the other to it, and slide the first leg out again. Then to the other side. In other words, slide, together, slide—back and forth to either side. Move from side to side with the arms swinging up, around over the head, down and side to side. Think of your arms and legs as coming from the navel and feel the downward pressure in your arms and legs.

FIVE: Stand with a wide base, one foot in front of the other, and relax the back knee down as far as possible, keeping the front foot down flat. Come up through the Center. Move the back leg to the front. The body pivots in the direction of the new back foot, making it the front foot, and the back knee relaxes down. Repeat.

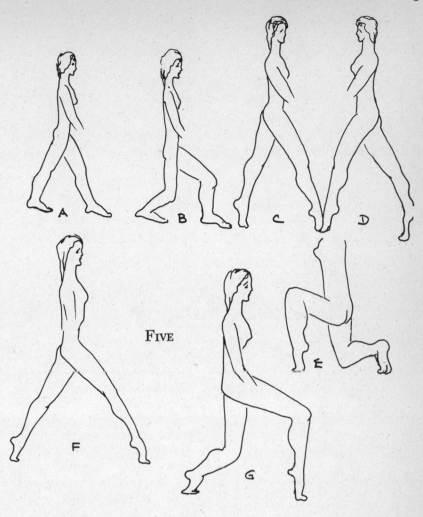

FIVE

continuous movement

SIX. TONGUES OF FLAME. Hang over heavily from the end of your spine. Feel as if you are hanging from a thread. Be sure to drop your head completely. As the torso rises, one hand moves up thumb side in, from the toes, between the legs, and up, cutting up the center of the body and up on a long stretch. The arm then extends out and down as the body moves straight down and over from the hips. Do the same with the other hand. As you go down, reach out as far as possible with the active arm, relaxing the other one completely. Stress the thumbs-in position.

SEVEN: Come up the same way with one arm and, at the highest point up, swing the arm around in a circle, pulling the body with it. Then reach out over and down. Repeat to one side for a while, then to the other side. A variation on this is to hang over from the end of the spine and bring both arms up close to the body. On the up-through, the arms start moving up and around to one side. The arms can start going around at any point in the up-through, until you are all the way up. Relax down and repeat.

Lesson Plan Thirty-Four

ONE

ONE: Your body is fire. Tuck in, knees bent and elbows close to sides, hands up and palms touching. One arm moves up slightly as the other moves down. Heels move in opposition—i.e., the left hand and right heel come up together. Intense, controlled holding-in of abdomen. As the left hand moves down, the right heel moves down. Fire is banked. But then the up draught becomes strong. The heels stamp down hard and one hand shoots upward. Your heels are the crackling fire; hands and head are flames. The fire of the feet mounts up through the body and your arms shoot up, one passing the other.

TWO: SUNSET FIRE. With feet apart and knees bent, extend your arms out to the sides on a horizontal plane. Work with resistance. Pull out through one arm to the side, then through the other. Let your knees give until you reach the floor, where you rest. Come up by stretching through an arm and leg on one side, pulling to that side and stretching to the other side, pulling slowly from side to side through the arms and knees, until you have risen in an upright position. Go down again. Feel and think of your body as the sun setting beyond the horizon in flaming bands of color.

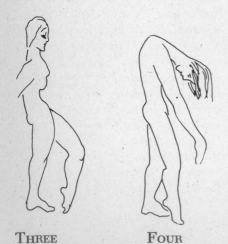

THREE   FOUR

THREE: WALKING IN HOT SAND. Well tucked in, control your body from the abdomen. Raise one leg as if on a spring and take a step with the foot barely touching the ground. It must go down, even though it burns, in order to progress. The other foot then comes forward slightly. When it touches, it recoils up from the sand, but it must come down with weight on it in order to free the other foot. Continue for a time.

FOUR: The sand has cooled slightly, but you are very tired. Your head and arms hang over from the Center. Your feet sink into the sand. A great effort is needed to pick up the weight of a leg. It lifts only with the lift of the back Center. Feel the alternation of the rising breath and lifting Center with gravity pulling down.

FIVE: You come upon a sparkling, very cold brook in the early morning. A toe goes into the water; it rebounds back from the knee, the foot contracting upward. Control is from the abdomen. The foot jumps back to meet the other and makes little jumps forward. The movement is much the same as the Hot Sand, but here the action is revitalizing. Repeat three or four times with each foot and then jump boldly in with both feet. Splash the water around.

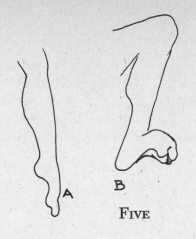

FIVE

SIX: Walk barefoot in a forest, feeling thorny growth underfoot. The sole of the foot contracts back and away. Put the foot down and step gingerly with the other foot. Concentrate on all parts of your feet feeling all sensations.

Lesson Plan Thirty-Five

ONE: Stretch.

TWO: Stand with feet together, heels touching. Raise one heel briskly as high as possible, letting it brush the other on the way down. Raise the other heel. Emphasize first the up, then later the down movement of the heels. The toes are the last to leave the floor. Alternate heels, till you lose the sense of which is up and which is down. Then turn on it, up, down, up, down.

THREE: STRIKING SPARKS OF FIRE. Keep well tucked-in and strike one heel against the earth

three times, then strike the other heel down three times. After a while alternate, only one strike to a side. Keep the feet turned out and strike out to the side. Turn your head to the side the heel is striking. This can develop into a great variety of movements. Try using various rhythms, such as Spanish, Hindu or peasant music.

FOUR: VULCAN. Your breath acts as bellows and a slight crossing and uncrossing of hands fans the fire. With one foot in front of the other, knees bent and your weight on the back foot, tuck in and draw into the back. Hold your hands down and crossed over the front knee. Hang your head over from the Center and breathe in. The hands uncross a bit and the head comes up somewhat. Breathe out. The hands cross and head hangs. Repeat breathing in and out four times. The fourth time is larger, and a fifth is explosive. Breathe in deep and full. The head comes up from the Center, arms expand out hori-

THREE

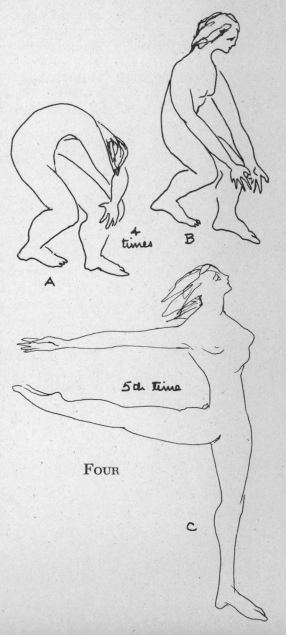

FOUR

zontally, and the back leg flies up to the back. The front knee straightens. Hold the position. A burst of energy expands your head, legs and arms out in five directions. The back leg dangles forward, your body curls in, the knees bend and the hands cross as you breathe out. The weight is on the back foot. Repeat.

FIVE: VULCAN HITTING METAL ON THE ANVIL.

The heel is a hammer, the floor is an anvil, the spirit is the metal, the chest is the bellows and the fire is in the lower pelvic center. As before, be aware of the breath. Hold your arms out to the sides horizontally and raise one leg slightly to the back. Breathe in as the arms come up overhead and the back leg moves forward, folding at the knee as it does so. Bring the knee up high in front and then stamp down on the heel as you breathe out. Transfer the weight to your front foot. Repeat.

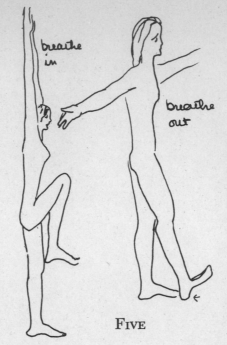

FIVE

SIX: Rest on the floor on your side, contracted in and feeling all warm. Roll over onto your back, expanding out in all directions. Do the scissor stretch and then return to a curled-up position. Roll up onto your knees and stand up. End with legs apart. Swing your arms up and down from side to side, one, two. On the third swing up, bring them over your head, around and down. Shift your weight as the arms move, first to one leg, then to the other. Then leap in half-turns as the arms go over the head. The knees relax as the arms come down.

SIX

Lesson Plan Thirty-Six

ONE: Start with a Jacob's Ladder stretch.

TWO: Rotary movements of the wrist and arm. Hold one arm up from the elbow. Circle the hand from the wrist, up around, down and up, and then drop it heavily. Repeat a few times. Stretch the arm out to the side at the shoulder height, continuing to revolve the wrist, faster and faster. Raise the forearm from the elbow and drop it heavily a few times. Try to feel a space at the elbow. Circle the whole lower arm around from the elbow a number of times. Shoot the arm down from the elbow, let it come up and shoot it down again. Repeat five or six times. Swing the arm around from the shoulder a number of times. Think of the back Center and shoot the arm forward from there. Then swing the arm from the shoulder up, out and around from the back Center. Repeat. Then do the complete exercise with the other arm.

THREE: Swing one arm in, out, and in and up and around to the back. The feet should be comfortably apart. Relax the knees with the swing and transfer your weight with movement of the arm. As it moves to the back, make a half-turn in that direction. Work with one arm for a while, then the other, then use both arms together but to alternate sides.

THREE

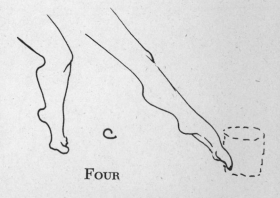

FOUR: Standing on one foot, raise the other foot and contract it, stretching the heel down. Drop the foot and repeat a number of times. Rotate the foot at the ankle. Kick the lower leg out from the knee to the side, as if kicking away a bucket. Repeat five or six times. Rotate the lower leg from the knee a number of times. Shoot the leg out to the side from the hip five or six times. Raising

FOUR

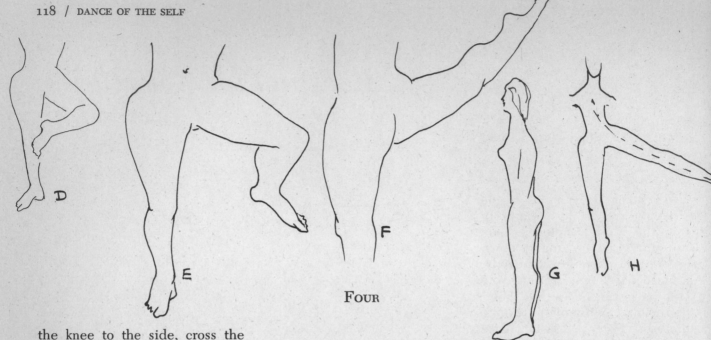

FOUR

the knee to the side, cross the lower leg over in front of the other thigh, then up, out and around to the back. Straighten the knee as the leg moves around. Lift the foot as high as possible to the back before bringing it down to the floor beside the other foot. Think of a high Center and shoot your leg out to the side from there as you hop on the other foot. Repeat the movement and then do the complete exercise with the other leg.

FIVE: Stand with one foot in front of the other. Then circle the front knee in, out to a full stretch, around to the back and down at a comfortable distance behind the front foot. Put your weight on the back foot. Alternate legs. Do this for some time, correlating it with the same kind of movement of the opposite arm.

SIX: Rest on the floor on your back, both knees to your chest. Bounce the lower legs up and down from the knees, occasionally kicking the buttocks. Then bounce, bounce one leg and shoot it straight up with the knee straight and heel stretched up, foot contracted. Then do same with other leg. Still lying flat on your back, do the Jacob's Ladder stretch on the floor, stretching up through the arms and trying to move in that direction. Do the same with the legs, making an effort to move in that direction. Roll onto your knees and come up to a standing position.

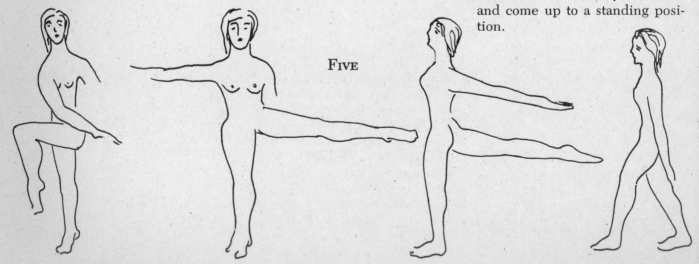

FIVE

SEVEN

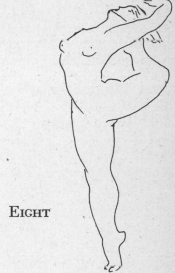

EIGHT

SEVEN: Start with a tucked-in position, heels together. Then half-sit on one leg, body contracted in, and move the other knee and elbow over to the side of the standing leg. Sling the arm and leg back out to their own side. The foot lands with emphasis as the body comes up through from the end of the spine, the up-through line extending out past the head. As the weight shifts, the arm is sent out horizontal and the opposite leg flies up to the side. The extended leg slowly comes to rest beside the other as the arm slowly comes down to the side and the chest moves up high. Then the Center contracts in as the other elbow and knee cross to the opposite side. Alternate a number of times. Then do it as a march. Walk, one, two, gather in, sling, stamp, up-through, draw together slowly and walk, one, two, etc.

EIGHT: Walk, one, two, gather in, sling out and around. Arm and leg fly around to the back. Let it become a large, circular turn.

Lesson Plan Thirty-Seven

ONE: Stretch

TWO: Circle shoulders, elbows and wrists in rotaries. Feet together, tuck in, one arm extended out horizontal. At the fullest reach out from the Center, bring the arm down, around, up and out, keeping it extended. Make a

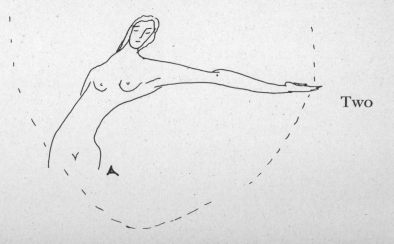

TWO

full circle. Then circle from the elbow and the wrist. Spend a long time with rotaries on one side, so that there is a long under-arm pull. The upper arm and back will shift out to the side beyond your hip and ankle. Repeat the rotaries on the other side; then work both sides together.

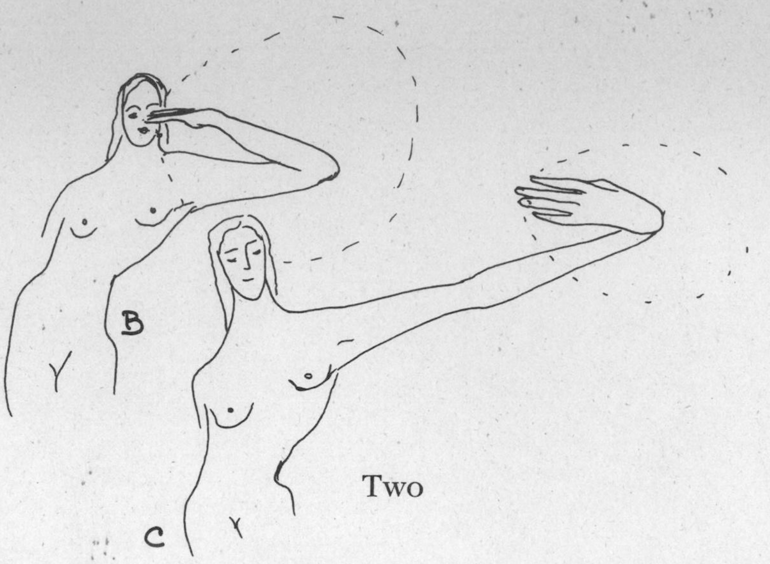

Two

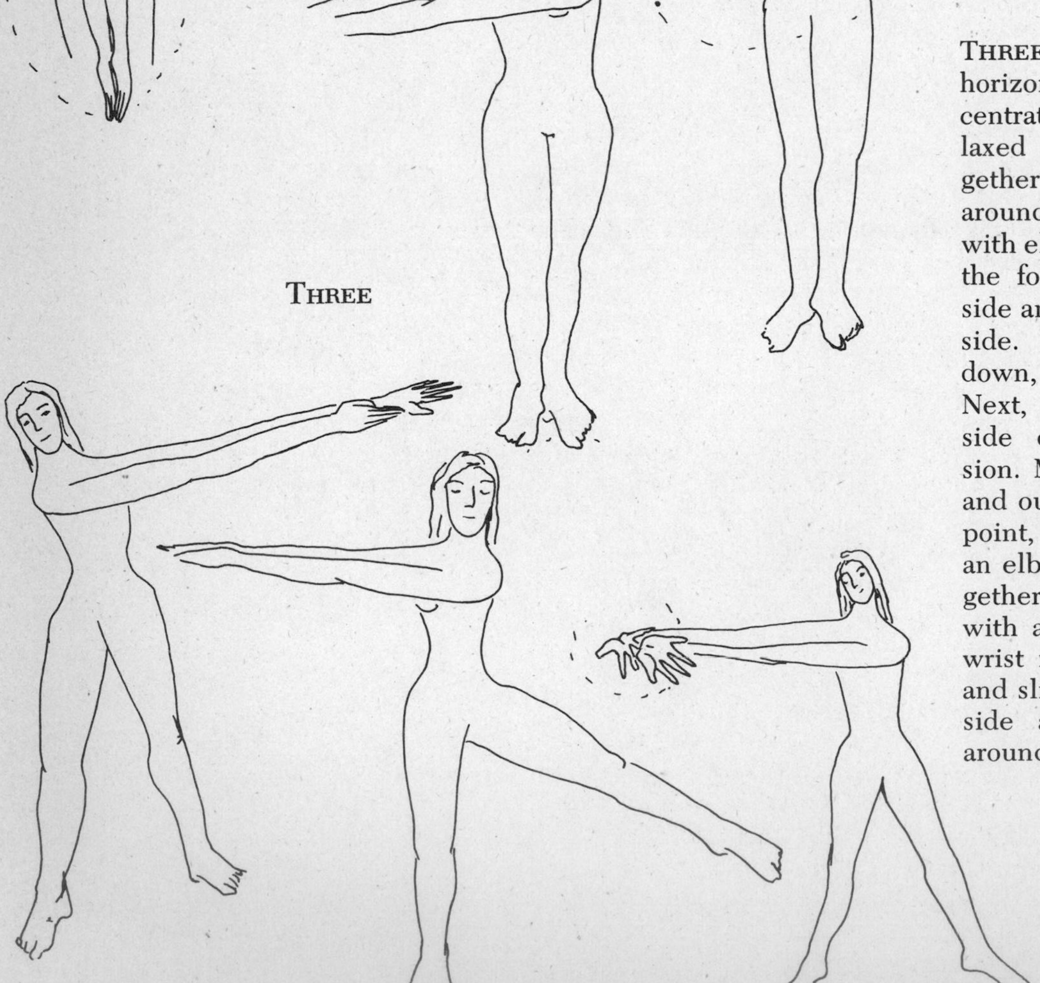

THREE

THREE: Extend both arms out horizontal to one side. Concentrate on keeping shoulders relaxed and down. Both arms together make large circles, down, around, up, out and down. Then, with elbows close together, circle the forearms around, up to the side and extend both arms to one side. Then circle the hands down, in, up and around. Repeat. Next, slide one foot out to the side opposite the arm extension. Move the arms up, around and out to the other side; at that point, bring the feet together. Do an elbow rotary with the feet together. Then step out to the side with arms extended and do the wrist rotary. Step back to place and slide the other foot out to its side and circle the arms up around and extended out. Repeat.

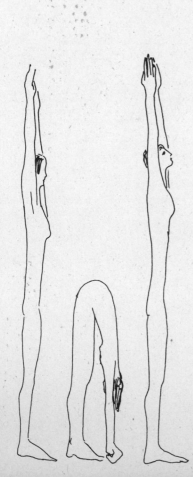

FOUR: Half-sit, well tucked-in, one foot a comfortable distance in front of the other. Think of going down a hill of soft mud. With the foot pulled up, feel carefully down with the heel of the front foot. Press down and then test the ground with the center of the foot. Press down, move onto the ball of the foot and press down again. Feel with the toes, press down and slowly, with pressure, move the foot back to the heel. Put your weight on that foot and allow the back foot to come up and steal forward. Repeat for some time, feeling the ground for sure footing.

FOUR

FIVE: Take a large step forward. Let the Center fall over the front knee and rebound up. Step, step, step and fall. Repeat. Sink to the floor, rest. Come up and move freely.

SIX: First one heel up, then the other. Keep thinking higher and higher through the head. Feel light and free, dancing delicately.

FIVE

Lesson Plan Thirty-Eight

ONE: Start with the Jacob's Ladder stretch, feeling the underarm taking the stretch. Then, as if holding on to a tree branch, pull down suddenly and forcefully, and, as forcefully, spring back up. Feel the underarm take the stretch. Repeat. You can think of this in another way as a jackknife being snapped open and shut.

ONE

stop short

TWO: Pull the arms out in front at shoulder level, back Center resisting. Tuck in completely. Feel a line of energy up through. Curve your arms, keeping them loose at the elbows. Feel the back Center continue to pull. On the up-through, lift heels alternately with your knees taking the lift. Resist the up-through, remain in at the back Center, and rest into the lower back. The knees leap higher and higher. Travel on it. When you wish to rest, pull with back Center and lower back against the forward pull of the arms and stop short, like a man pulling horses to a sudden stop. Repeat.

Two

THREE: Stretch out on the floor on your stomach with legs together. Rest your forehead on the floor. Feel as if you were sinking into hot sand. Imagine you are a seal, arms like flippers, legs like a tail. Rest completely. Feel an impulse at back Center drawing one arm up, then the other, until you are propped on your elbows, palms resting down. With eyes wide open, look at the floor, then to the horizon. As if following clouds with your eyes, look as far up and backward as you can. Slowly lower yourself to an outstretched position by reversing the manner of coming up. Repeat five times and end resting on elbows. Turn your head to the left, following clouds with your eyes up around to the right, up and back to the left, down. Allow the head to hang, resting, then repeat to the right. Resting on your forearms, draw yourself up higher by the same method until your weight is on your hands, with the elbows straight. Repeat down and up a number of times. By raising your buttocks up, you come up on your hands and knees. Sit back on your heels and fold the body forward, arms stretched out in front.

back center lifts one arm

THREE

FOUR: Rise and fall from the back Center, higher each time until you are sitting up on your heels. Tuck in, push through at the crotch, lift at the Center and come up onto your knees. Still tightly tucked-in, lift the Center again, sway back, drop your elbows to the floor at the back and rest your head on the floor. Push forward at your crotch and lift your chest up, with the top of your head on the floor. Repeat down and up.

FIVE: Stand with legs apart, tuck in and raise both arms up to one side. Move in a huge under-arc from one leg to the other, knees giving and arms swinging from side to side. Do this three times, then raise your arms over your head as you leap and turn. Land facing the original direction.

FOUR

Lesson Plan Thirty-Nine

ONE: Start with the Jacob's Ladder stretch.

TWO: Tuck in, rest into the back Center and relax your knees slightly. Raise your arms at an oblique angle, holding them up gently. As the up-through releases itself up, let the arms come down. Tuck in again as the arms come up, thus creating a passing motion. Repeat many times.

TWO

THREE: Tuck in. Raise one arm as you think of breathing out under the armpit. Move the upper torso out in the direction of the armpit. Raise the other arm and move the torso in that direction as you think of feeling the air moving to that side.

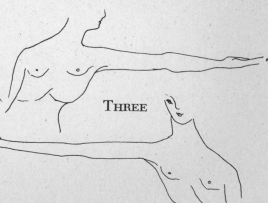

THREE

FOUR: Standing on one leg, swing the other leg forward, back and forward, back and forward. The standing foot hops forward on the final forward swing. Hold the leg up in front as long as possible, then release down and swing the other leg. Continue for some time.

FIVE: Stand up high, tuck in. With one foot directly in front of the other, think up through the head. Breathe in, move the front Center over the front foot and come up on the ball of that foot, bringing the other foot slowly forward. Come down stressing the heel of the back foot. Keep your head high, knees straight and a strong tuck-in so that there is real body tension. Move the front Center across the ball of the front foot. Repeat the rhythm for some time.

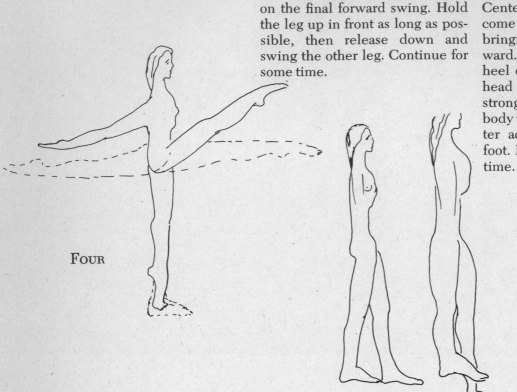

FOUR

FIVE

SIX: Stand with legs apart and tuck in, head up. Relax your shoulders and keep your arms close to your body. Let the knees give, as you shift your weight from leg to leg in an under-arc. Let the arms take up the rhythm. Move from left to right to left, then come up on the left side, drawing the right leg in close. Extend your right arm out to the side at shoulder level and turn your head in that direction while the body turns to the left. Go down into your left knee and tuck in as your right leg stretches out to the side. Let the rhythm flow from left to right and repeat.

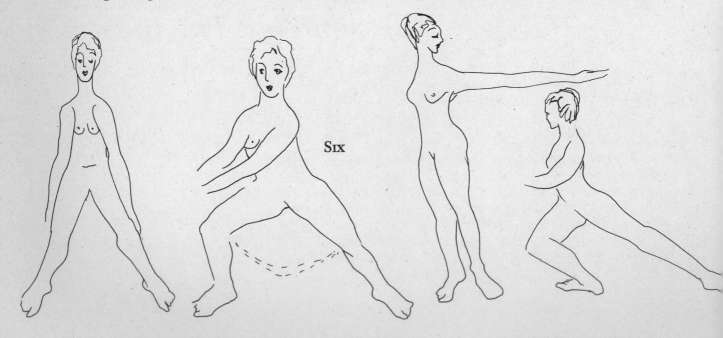

SIX

SEVEN: Stand on one leg and raise the other to the front, up high with a straight knee. Turn the raised foot from the ankle in a complete rotary. Lower the leg until the heel touches the floor and then slowly put your weight on it and lift the other leg. Repeat.

EIGHT: Move the hips from side to side, then circle them in a rotary. Reverse the direction and repeat.

NINE: Circle the upper torso in a rotary. Feel air moving from front Center to underarm to back Center to underarm. Continue around. Reverse the rotary direction. Do not twist to either side.

TEN: Tuck in and assume a half-sitting position. Step, step, take a

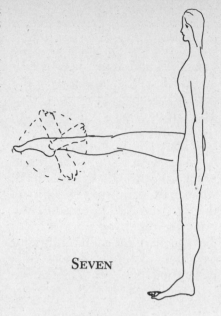

SEVEN

small leap, then step, step and a larger leap, until it builds up into tremendous leaps with the Center high and the back leg flying.

ELEVEN: Tuck in, half-sit. Step, step, going in circles and allowing energy to leak away until you are almost on the floor. When the ankles give, fall in a heap. Rise up, stand with feet together and repeat in the opposite direction, taking small steps.

TWELVE: Lie on the floor, legs, arms and head stretched wide apart like a starfish. Draw all five points together. Then bring them up in the air and hold before returning them slowly to the floor, one at a time. Relax, stretch and repeat.

THIRTEEN: Stand up high with heels together. Move constantly up on toes and down on heels, keeping the heels together. Think up through the head. Allow the arms to move freely. Dance on the movement of your breath.

Lesson Plan Forty

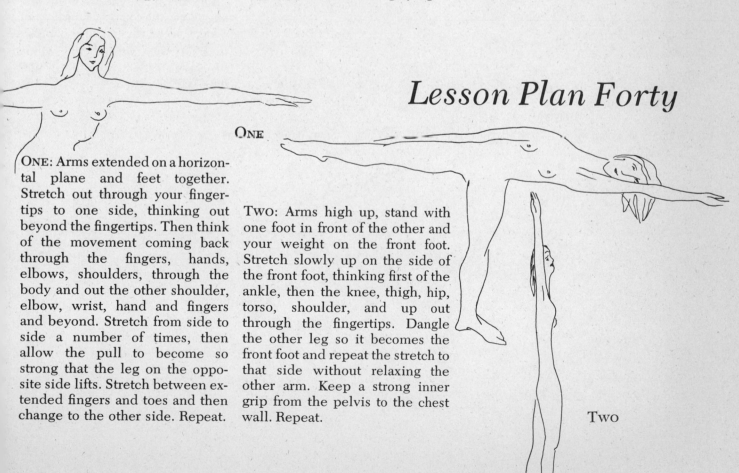

ONE

TWO

ONE: Arms extended on a horizontal plane and feet together. Stretch out through your fingertips to one side, thinking out beyond the fingertips. Then think of the movement coming back through the fingers, hands, elbows, shoulders, through the body and out the other shoulder, elbow, wrist, hand and fingers and beyond. Stretch from side to side a number of times, then allow the pull to become so strong that the leg on the opposite side lifts. Stretch between extended fingers and toes and then change to the other side. Repeat.

TWO: Arms high up, stand with one foot in front of the other and your weight on the front foot. Stretch slowly up on the side of the front foot, thinking first of the ankle, then the knee, thigh, hip, torso, shoulder, and up out through the fingertips. Dangle the other leg so it becomes the front foot and repeat the stretch to that side without relaxing the other arm. Keep a strong inner grip from the pelvis to the chest wall. Repeat.

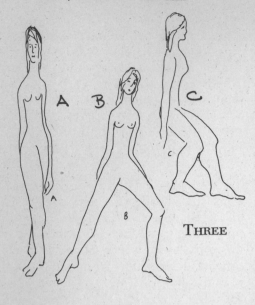

THREE

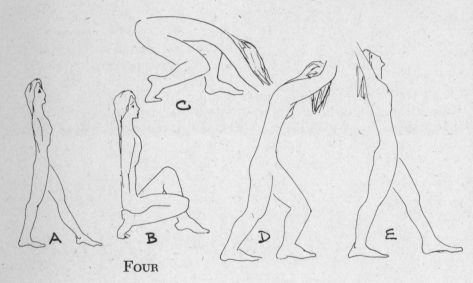

FOUR

the weight to the front foot, come up through and stretch the back leg out to the side. Repeat.

THREE: Stand with one foot in front of the other, the toes of the back foot touching the front heel. Tuck in and keep the body upright, with your weight on the front foot. Let the back leg lift out to the side in a long stretch and bring it down so that your feet are well apart with your weight on the foot you just lowered. Then bring the other leg up to it with toes touching the heel. Shift your weight onto the back foot in a half-sitting position. Then move

FOUR: With one foot in front of the other, comfortably apart, take three long steps forward. Tuck in, keeping your body upright, then sink down so that the buttocks come down onto the back heel. Let the Center move forward and down over the front knee and then raise the Center up, with your head and arms held high. Repeat.

FIVE: Stand and raise one leg slowly with the sole of the foot against the inside of the standing leg. Slide the foot up from the ankle to the knee. Turn your leg out and extend it to the side, with toes pointed. Then drop the lower leg from the knee and move it back, around, in and under the thigh and then out at a stretched diagonal. Let the foot come to the floor. Move diagonally forward through that knee, draw the back leg to the front, and repeat the stretch with the other leg.

FIVE

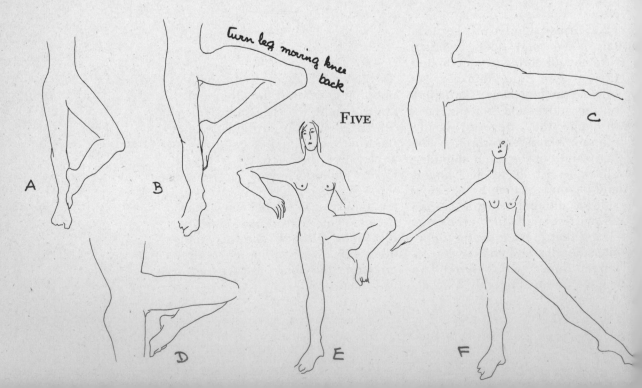

SIX: On the floor with knees up, squidge the lower back into hot sand.

SEVEN: Come to your feet and dance, forcing your breath up high in the chest.

Lesson Plan Forty-One

ONE: With the right leg forward, pull the right arm to the front and the left arm to the back so that they are at shoulder level. The back arm comes up and the forward arm moves down. Maintain the stretch. The left leg moves to the front as the left arm comes over to the front horizontal plane and the right arm rotates to the horizontal plane in back. Continue these stretches.

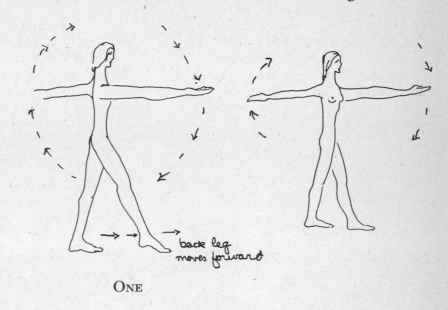

ONE

TWO: Force an up-and-down current. Start with legs apart and arms out horizontal. Grip tightly with the pelvis and lift the chest as one leg crosses over in front of the other leg. Push the chest down as your weight goes onto the front foot. Raise the chest up as the back leg moves out to the side so that you are standing with legs apart. Go down into the knees and press the chest down. Then raise the chest up as you cross the leg over to the front again. Continue moving to one side across the room and then go in the other direction.

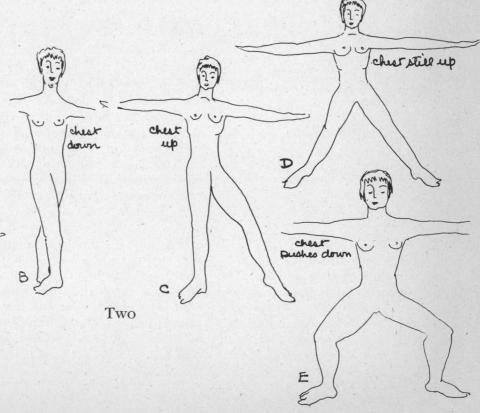

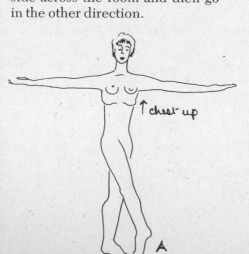

THREE: Repeat the above adding a turn after each complete movement. The arms come over head and you make two half-turns, ending with legs apart.

FOUR: Stand with legs apart. Stretch up high, to the fullest reach. Force the body down from the Center. The arms come apart and settle down. The torso is kept erect. The heels remain down as the knees give and you force the body down as low as possible. Then rise up to the greatest stretch. Repeat.

THREE

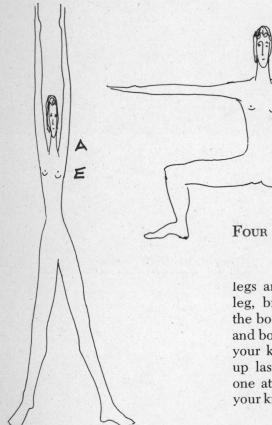

FOUR

legs and head. Slowly raise one leg, bringing the knee close to the body, then raise the other leg and both arms, one at a time. Hug your knees and bring your head up last. Slowly unfold all parts, one at a time. Repeat. Roll onto your knees and come up.

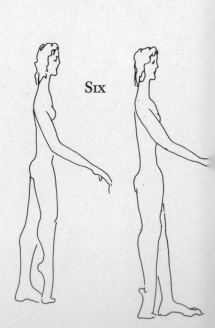

SIX

FIVE: Drop down to the floor, then come circling around and up to the full stretch. Drop down and come up a few times. Drop to the floor and rest on your side in a curled-up position. Turn onto your back and stretch out arms,

SIX: Against resistance, raise one foot onto toes and lower it slowly. Shove the other foot ahead with a force that comes from clenched buttocks. Move the heel in front of and touching the big toe of the other foot. Repeat raising the front foot.

SEVEN: This movement is done on breath pulsation. Stand with feet together and breathe in. Step out to one side and raise your arms up to shoulder level in a soft motion, legs and feet turned out. Breathe out and sink into your knees as your arms come down and cross in front. Breathe in and step together again, repeating the movement to the same side several times. Then repeat toward the other side. Note: The right foot always moves to its side when moving to the right on the down breath. The left foot comes to it on the up breath. Reverse for the other direction.

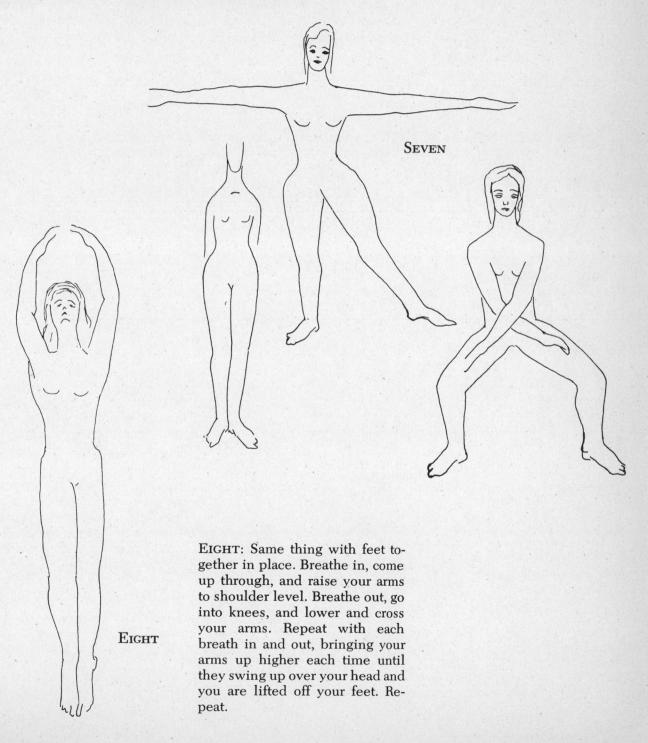

SEVEN

EIGHT

EIGHT: Same thing with feet together in place. Breathe in, come up through, and raise your arms to shoulder level. Breathe out, go into knees, and lower and cross your arms. Repeat with each breath in and out, bringing your arms up higher each time until they swing up over your head and you are lifted off your feet. Repeat.

Lesson Plan Forty-Two

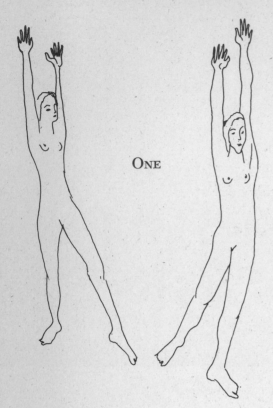

ONE

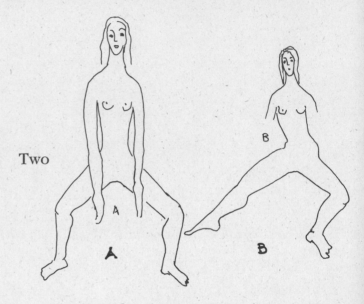

ONE: A complete stretch up, first with one arm, then the other. On the stretch of one arm, move the opposite leg forward and out on a diagonal. Feel the transfer of the stretch take place under the arm.

TWO: Body erect, legs apart and bent at the knees. Move through your hips to one side until the other leg straightens. Shift back to the other side. Repeat.

TWO

A

B

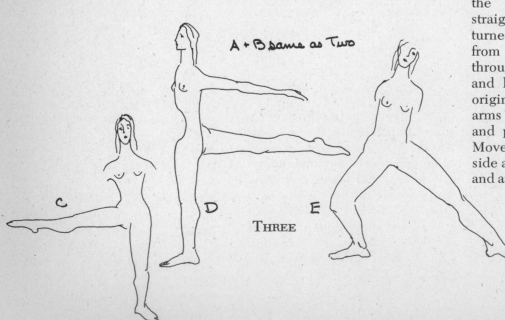

A + B same as Two

C   D   E

THREE

THREE: This is the same exercise with the addition of raising the straightened leg to the side and moving it and the opposite arm to the back as the other knee straightens. The raised leg is turned out. The arm moves back from the shoulder. Push forward through the pelvis and let the arm and leg swing forward to their original positions, legs apart and arms at the sides. Bend the knees and press the foot to the floor. Move through the hip to the other side and repeat with the other leg and arm.

FOUR: One foot in front of the other. Keeping the knees straight, lift the front leg to the side and around to the back and down to the floor diagonally behind the other foot. The body follows with the underarm leading and the chest raised high. Pivot so that the other leg is to the back. Now bring the back leg and the arm on that side out and around to the front and pull the body forward on a long line with the arm extended. Raise the chest high and the body will come upright. The back leg dangles forward. Lift it up and move it out to the side and around. Repeat.

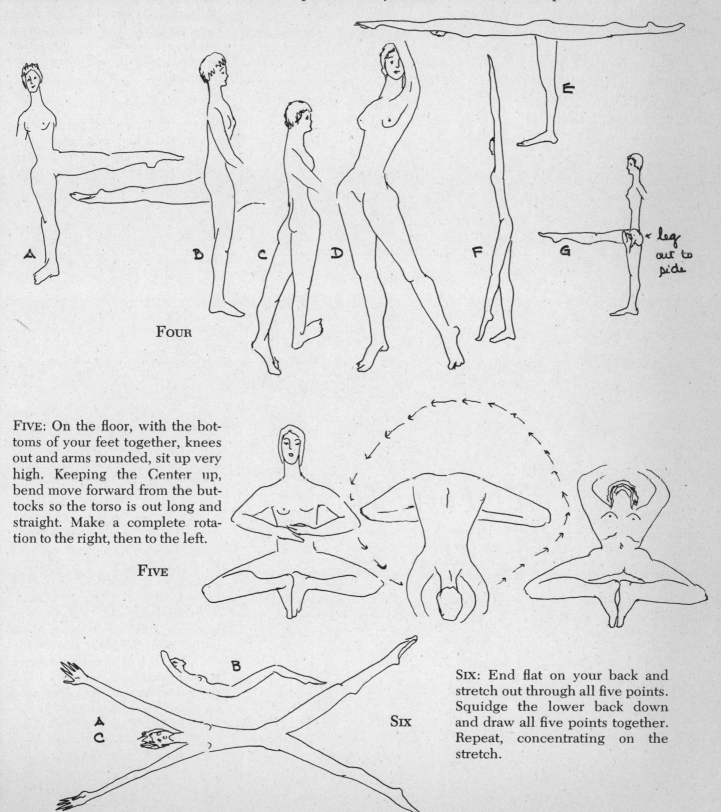

FOUR

FIVE: On the floor, with the bottoms of your feet together, knees out and arms rounded, sit up very high. Keeping the Center up, bend move forward from the buttocks so the torso is out long and straight. Make a complete rotation to the right, then to the left.

FIVE

SIX

SIX: End flat on your back and stretch out through all five points. Squidge the lower back down and draw all five points together. Repeat, concentrating on the stretch.

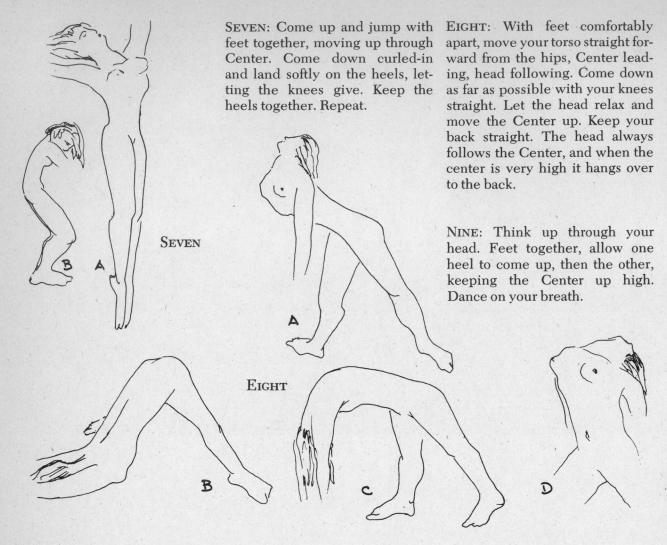

SEVEN: Come up and jump with feet together, moving up through Center. Come down curled-in and land softly on the heels, letting the knees give. Keep the heels together. Repeat.

EIGHT: With feet comfortably apart, move your torso straight forward from the hips, Center leading, head following. Come down as far as possible with your knees straight. Let the head relax and move the Center up. Keep your back straight. The head always follows the Center, and when the center is very high it hangs over to the back.

NINE: Think up through your head. Feet together, allow one heel to come up, then the other, keeping the Center up high. Dance on your breath.

SEVEN

EIGHT

Lesson Plan Forty-Three

ONE

ONE: Stretch one arm up and stretch the leg on that side forward on a diagonal, with the leg turned out and toes pointed. Transfer your weight to the forward leg and stretch the arm out to that side. Allow the knee of the standing leg to bend, and move the stretched arm forward. Bend the other arm at the elbow and move it to the back. Slide the forward foot still further forward before moving your body up to it. Repeat on the other foot.

TWO: With one foot in front of the other and arms folded to the back, elbows shoulder-high and as close together as possible, rest your head back from the Center, keeping the Center high. Movement comes from lifting the Center. Elbows and head remain as they are as one leg lifts to the back, as high as possible. Hold and then let the leg come down and to the front. Transfer your weight onto it. Lift the other leg back and repeat. The head comes up as the weight transfers.

THREE: With elbows and head remaining to the back, move your front leg up and around to the side, extended from the hip, and then down to the back. Turn the body to follow. Then move the other leg in the same pattern.

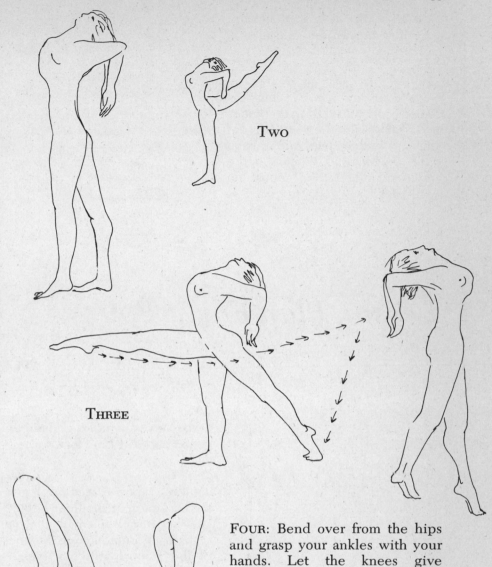

FOUR: Bend over from the hips and grasp your ankles with your hands. Let the knees give slightly. Raise one hip and straighten the knee on that side. Repeat on the other side. Hang over for a time and then come up and repeat.

FIVE: Stand tall with legs apart comfortably and bend over from the hips, hands to the floor. Drop the buttocks to the floor and sit tall. Then raise the buttocks high and let the torso come down with a straight back as you straighten your knees. Repeat the whole movement a few times. Then bend over again, raising your buttocks high, and grasp your ankles. Take a small leap as you come up. Repeat several times.

SIX: Sit on the floor with legs out together. Move from side to side out through the elbows.

SEVEN: Lie on one side, legs extended together. Draw the knees up slowly and then stretch the legs out with a snap, one to each side, diagonally. Repeat on the other side, and then repeat on your back.

SIX

SEVEN

EIGHT: Stand and move your head from the Center, backward and forward. Let the Center move first and the head follow. Dance with the head moving from the Center and legs dangling from Center.

Lesson Plan Forty-Four

ONE: THE JACOB'S LADDER STRETCH.

TWO: Move shoulders and tail together backward and forward.

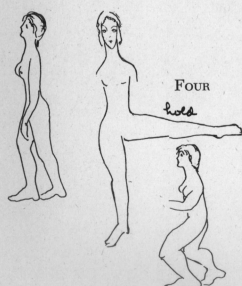

TWO

FOUR

hold

THREE: Opposite arm and leg to the back, arm at shoulder height, and feet turned out with the toe of the back foot touching the heel of the front foot. Your weight should be on your front foot. When the arm has pulled back as far as possible, you will feel a pinch at the back shoulder which will release the back arm and leg out and around to the front, heel and wrist leading. Repeat using other arm and leg.

FOUR: Start with a tuck-in and one foot in front of the other, weight on the front foot. Move the back leg out to the side and around to take the place in front. The other foot jumps slightly to the back. Come down softly on the whole front foot and move on it. Do the same from front to back.

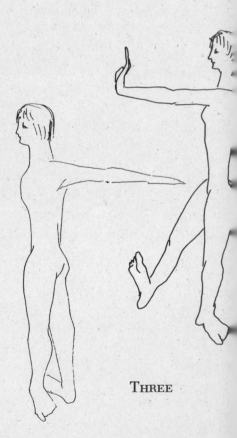

THREE

FIVE: On the floor, sit tall with straight legs and feet together. Move your torso around in a large circle. Reverse the direction. Repeat to both sides a number of times.

SIX

SIX: Lie on your back, throw your feet back over your head to the floor and stretch your legs out straight, resting on your shoulders. Pull to one side with one knee to the floor. Press down on your elbow on that side and turn your head so that the cheek comes to the floor. Pull through the stretched leg. You will turn a somersault, landing on one knee with the other leg stretched out behind you. Repeat to the other side.

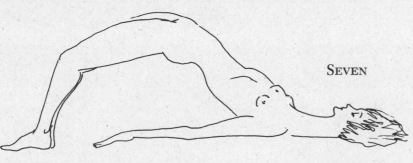

SEVEN

SEVEN: Lie on your back, knees up and feet on the floor. Push your crotch up as high as possible. Keep your arms at your sides on the floor. Starting at the neck, slowly lower yourself to the floor, one vertebra at a time, resisting with the crotch. Feel your back ironing itself out against the floor. Repeat.

EIGHT: Standing with one foot in front of the other on parallel lines, front toe pointed, exhale deeply. Sink down on the back leg, keeping the body upright. Feel an undercurrent go from the back foot to the front foot and up the front. The line of rhythm goes up from the front leg through the torso and out the head. The back leg moves to the front with the heel leading, pushing against the floor. Point the toes as you press your shoulders down, and move the arm on the side of the forward leg up. Turn it forward at the wrist to lower it and sink down on the back leg. Repeat.

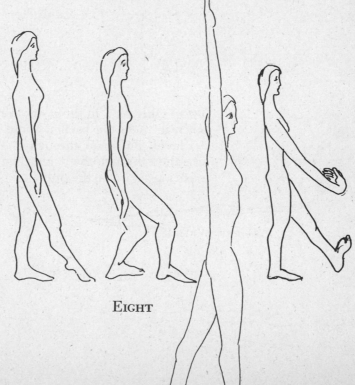

EIGHT

Lesson Plan Forty-Five

ONE: Stand with feet together and stretch your arms up. Pull forward from the hips, keeping your knees and torso straight. When you are as far forward as possible, bend the knees and pull your arms down and to the back from the shoulders. Push forward at the crotch as the torso rises. Keep your arms moving up at the back. Pinch the arms together when they reach shoulder level, bring them up high overhead and stretch. Repeat.

ONE

TWO: One foot in front of the other, arms to the back at shoulder level. Pull back through one arm, then through the other, then move backward on the pull.

move to back on it

TWO

move up and down through back center

A   B

THREE

C

THREE

THREE: With one foot in front of the other a comfortable distance, sink down over your front knee and then to the floor, the back Center pushing forward and down. Raise the Center up first, then come up on an up-through, head high, one foot in front of the other, weight on the back foot. The front leg lifts up to hip height, circles around with a straight knee, and comes down in back. Weight is on the front foot. Repeat. Feel all the movement start at the back Center. Rise and fall with it.

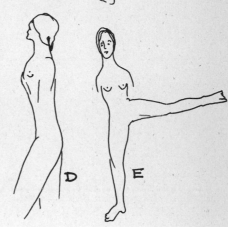

D   E

FOUR: Sit on the floor with the soles of your feet together and torso erect. Come forward from the end of spine to the right and then to the left. Do this a number of times.

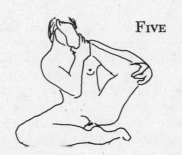

FIVE

FIVE: Seated as before, grasp a knee with one hand and the ankle with the other and try to bring your foot to your forehead. Keep your back and head erect. Repeat with other leg.

SIX: Stand with feet apart. Drop your buttocks straight down as your knees give. Push forward through the knees, then through the crotch and come up, keeping the chest high and letting your head and arms hang off to the back. Bring your head up and repeat.

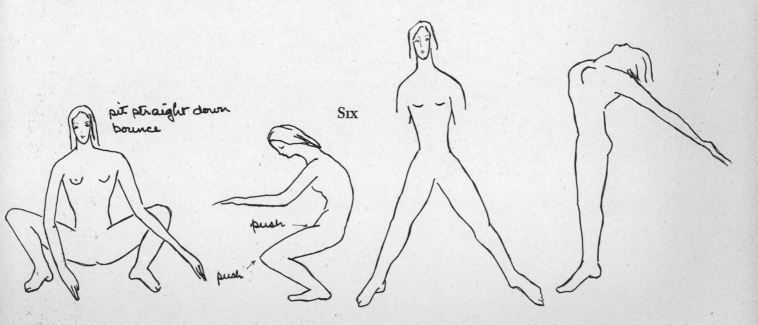

sit straight down bounce

SIX

push

push

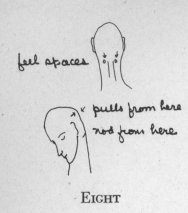

feel spaces

pulls from here
nod from here

EIGHT

SEVEN: Feet apart, bring the left foot in to the right foot, slide the right foot out to its side, and step with the left foot again to the right foot. Then the right foot jumps out to the side as the left foot leaps over it and the movement becomes a half-turn. Repeat to the other side with the left foot doing the sliding.

EIGHT: Up through the head, push your chin down in and arch your neck back as if you were a horse. Locate the two places where your neck joins your head; feel the key spaces. Allow your head to nod from the spaces, feeling the pull at the back of the head.

NINE: Stand with one foot in front of the other, and push your chin in, pressing back against the spaces at the back of your neck. Keep pressing back so far that the front foot falls backward and your weight shifts back onto it. Come up through and repeat.

Lesson Plan Forty-Six

ONE: Standing with feet apart and hands clasped over your head, pull up through one elbow, with your weight on that side. Slide the opposite leg across to the stretched side and bring it forward. Move the stretched elbow over toward the other side, stretching from under the arm. Keep your hands clasped, bring them down and twist your body to the back. Bend over forward at the furthest twist to the back. Start coming up and twist even more. Move your weight onto the front foot and come up slowly, the back leg moving out to the side. Then repeat the elbow stretch from the beginning on the other side.

TWO: Repeat the exercise above, without the forward bend. At the furthest twist to the back, stretch your arms out and bring the front leg around behind the back leg. Pivot and bend over at the shoulders, dropping the head. Repeat to the other side.

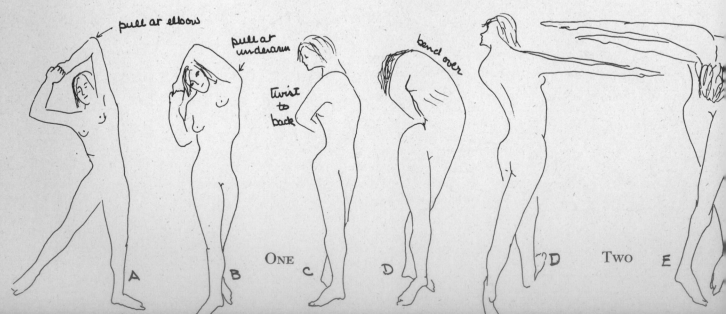

pull at elbow

pull at underarm

Twist to back

bend over

ONE   A   B   C   D   D   TWO   E

THREE: Yawn with clenched fists. Fold one arm up behind your head and keep it there as long as possible while you stretch, twist and bend to the back. Change to the other side. Continue yawning through this movement.

FOUR: Leap up to a full stretch and collapse to the floor, completely relaxed. Count one, two, leap up and return to the floor. Repeat a few times.

same as Lesson 45 #3 but from back center out through elbows

SEVEN: Then stand, relaxing the head down and feel the movement from the back Center come up and out through the shoulders and elbows, move up high, over, down and up. When they are up high, move up and down on the ball of front foot. Repeat several times and then, on toes, move the back leg to the front. Transfer your weight and repeat.

ONE

THREE

FIVE: Come up and move freely, feeling spontaneous impulses at the Center.

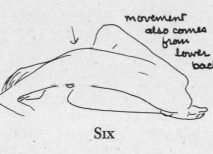

movement also comes from lower back

SIX

EIGHT: Run one, two, three to stoop, and leap in the air, always leading with the same foot. Then change and repeat with the other foot.

SIX: Repeat Exercise Three of Lesson Forty-Five.

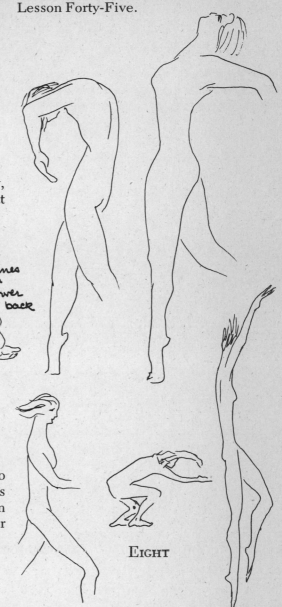

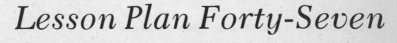

EIGHT

Lesson Plan Forty-Seven

ONE: Stand with one foot in front of the other and your weight on the front foot. Hold elbows up. Stretch the opposite elbow out over the front foot. Do not strain, but let the pull come from the shoulder. Release the back leg to the front and relax the shoulder pull. Move forward, alternating elbows.

TWO: Feet turned out, heel of front foot touching toe of back foot, body erect and knees bent. The back heel comes up and moves around the other heel and settles down in front. Repeat many times.

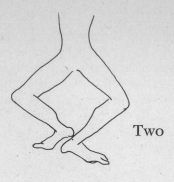

TWO

THREE

THREE: With your feet wide apart and your torso erect, move out from side to side through the knees, dipping lower and lower as your weight shifts. Then up in the same manner. Be sure the heels remain on the floor.

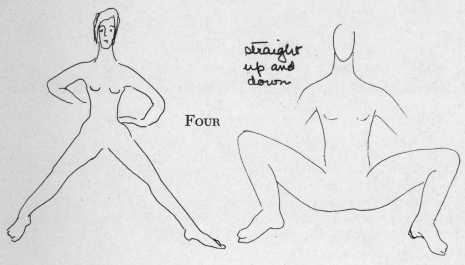

FOUR

straight up and down

FOUR: Feet wide apart, body erect and arms rounded, press out through both your knees and sit straight down. Come up and repeat several times. Keep the movement flowing.

FIVE: Jump in place many times, bringing the heels down softly. Let the knees give, and curl in as you land.

SIX: Lie on the floor and do a scissors stretch, first slowly and then quickly, turning over each time. Roll the length of the room, then scissor-stretch back the other way across the room.

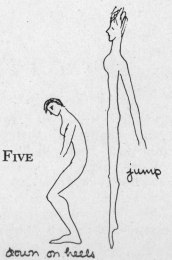

FIVE

jump

down on heels

SEVEN: Roll onto your knees, bring one foot to the front and come up through the back Center, up through the head, and stand. Dangle the back leg forward, shift your weight onto it and step, step. Bend the front knee, move the Center down over it and relax. Then come up through and repeat.

Lesson Plan Forty-Eight

ONE: Start with a Jacob's Ladder stretch.

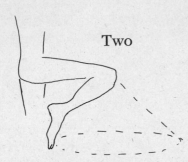

TWO

TWO: Lift one leg and twirl it from the knee. Repeat. Then repeat with the other leg.

THREE: Circle one foot from the ankle, emphasizing the arc up. Then circle the other foot.

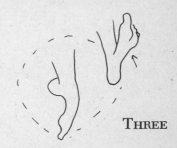

THREE

FOUR: With one foot comfortably in front of the other, bend the front knee and press back against the back knee. Move out through the hip of the bent knee side. Then bend the body toward the straight leg. Press down on the foot of the bent leg and feel a line of energy come up through. The back leg moves to the front. Repeat.

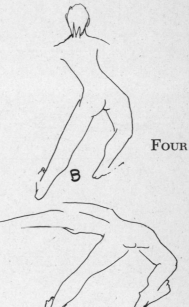

FOUR

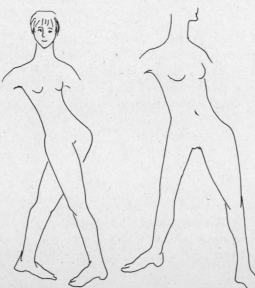

FIVE

FIVE: With legs slightly apart and feet turned out, move out through one hip. The opposite leg crosses over in front, and then the back leg steps out to the side as you move further out through the hip. Continue moving out to that side for a while, then repeat to the other side.

SIX: One foot in front of the other, up on toes, arms out at shoulder height to the side of the front leg. Come down on the back heel and move the front leg across in front, toes pointed. Shift your weight onto the front foot as the other foot makes a large step out to the side, uncrossing the legs. Bend that knee, as you extend the other leg straight out to the side. Bend the torso, arms stretched out, to the side of the straight leg. Then rise up, bring the other leg forward and move your arms out to the other side. Come up on your toes and repeat alternating sides.

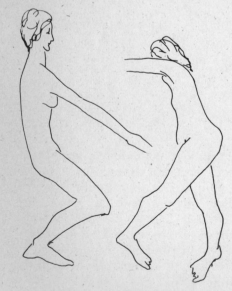

SEVEN: Feet somewhat apart, jump up and land softly on your toes, then heels, with knees turned out and bent. Make a half-turn to the back through one hip. Release the back leg out to the side and jump again. Turn through the other hip to the other side. Repeat.

EIGHT: Yawn, stretch, pull and twist. Then yawn with your shoulders up and your head hanging heavily.

NINE: Pull your shoulders down and open your eyes wide. Roll your eyes until you have the sensation that they are rolling around the top of your head.

Lesson Plan Forty-Nine

ONE: Stand with feet together and elbows at your sides, with the backs of your hands together at waist level, wrists touching. Move your hands up so that the knuckles touch each other and the wrists separate. Continue to roll the fingers through and bring elbows together as the hands unfold out with fingers curling upward. Push up with the heels of your hands. The arms separate as they move up into a stretch. Turn the hands down at the wrists so that the tips of the fingers meet overhead, hands horizontal. Push down with the fingers until the backs of the wrists touch. Continue pushing down with wrists together until the elbows reach the waist. Then begin the movement up again. Repeat until the pattern is well established. Then, as the hands are moving up, lift one leg out to the side. When the fingers come together overhead, lower the leg to the floor but keep it stretched out to the side. As the hands move down, transfer your weight to the stretched leg and move the other leg toward it. You continue to move to the side of the stretched leg. After a while, stretch the other leg and move to the other side.

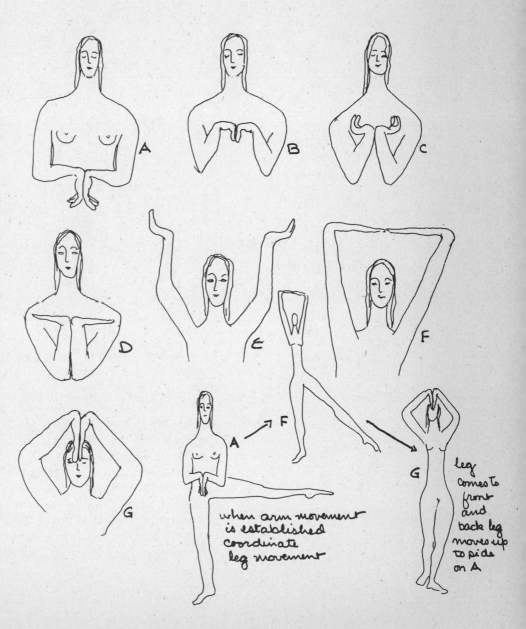

when arm movement is established coordinate leg movement

leg comes to front and back leg moves up to side on A

TWO: Keeping one leg in place, step forward and back with the other leg to the count of one, two. Do it twice on one side. Then step forward, step, step and repeat to the other side. Do this for some time. Opposite arm and leg are coordinated. Keep your Center high and feel the elastic tension of your body.

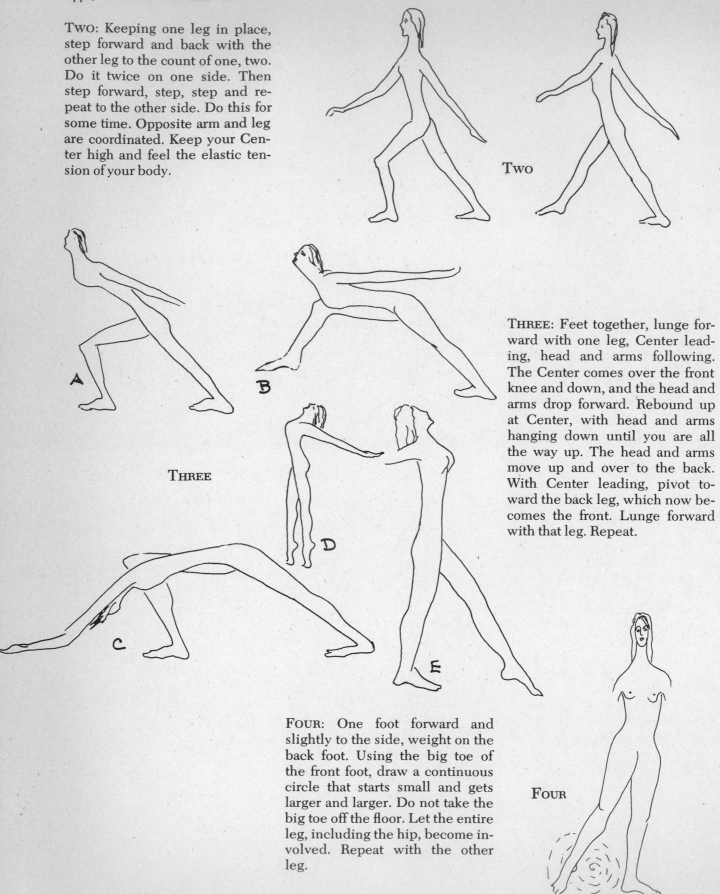

Two

A

B

THREE

C

D

E

THREE: Feet together, lunge forward with one leg, Center leading, head and arms following. The Center comes over the front knee and down, and the head and arms drop forward. Rebound up at Center, with head and arms hanging down until you are all the way up. The head and arms move up and over to the back. With Center leading, pivot toward the back leg, which now becomes the front. Lunge forward with that leg. Repeat.

FOUR: One foot forward and slightly to the side, weight on the back foot. Using the big toe of the front foot, draw a continuous circle that starts small and gets larger and larger. Do not take the big toe off the floor. Let the entire leg, including the hip, become involved. Repeat with the other leg.

FOUR

FIVE: Lie on the floor and do the scissors stretch, rolling from one end of the room to the other and back.

SIX: One foot pointed in front of the other, assume a strong tuck-in so that you feel your whole body in tension. Think up through. Put your weight on the back foot and bring the back heel up against resistance. Press against the back of the knee, putting stress at the back of your leg where it joins the buttocks. Transfer your weight to the front leg with the heel of the front foot coming down against resistance. Feel the resistance in the back leg as it moves to the front. Repeat.

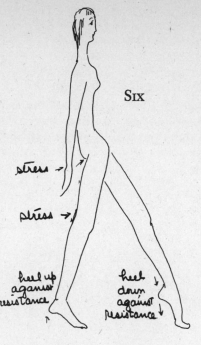

SIX

stress →
stress →
heel up against resistance
heel down against resistance

SEVEN: One foot in front of the other, step through with the back foot, step, step, and kick up the front leg. Then kick the back leg forward so that both feet leap and pass in a scissor kick. Repeat, starting with the other foot.

EIGHT: Same as Nine, Lesson Forty-Eight.

SEVEN

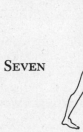

ONE

Lesson Plan Fifty

ONE: Stand with one foot in front of the other and repeat the Jacob's Ladder stretch several times with opposite leg and arm stretching. The ankles brush as the feet pass each other in a stretched walk.

TWO: Feet together, stand up very tall and lift one heel and then the other continuously. Stretch up through your head, and the heel movements quicken. Think of sun sparkling on water. Turn on it.

THREE: In a half-sitting position, move one foot forward and lift the leg high, out around in a circle to the back. It comes down, then forward with an extended stretch through the big toe, brushing the other foot in passing. Put your weight on the front foot. Bring the other foot forward and lift it up and around. Repeat.

FOUR: With one foot in front of the other, move the front leg as if it dangled from the hip in a circle that gets larger and larger. Describe the circle with the toes. Repeat, then repeat with the other leg.

FIVE: Feet together, keep the knees straight as you bend straight out from the hips and down. Then let the legs separate and the knees give and swing your body to the right, to the left, then back around to the right and up to a high stretch and down on the left side to the center. Bounce the torso down from the hips a few times and come straight up. Bring your feet together and repeat to the other side. Repeat.

after first complete movement swing starts to other side

FIVE

SIX: Lying on your back, stretch out all five points and then draw them together. Release them out simultaneously. Stretch and draw all five points together again, then release point by point. Repeat. Squidge the lower back around as if in soft sand. Yawn.

SEVEN: On your feet, half-sit. Extend your arms out, rounded and somewhat down. Move them to one side, down and up to the other side. Straighten your legs as the arms come up. Move the arms down, around, up and over the head and down. Repeat, reversing the direction of the arm movement. Come up on your toes as the arms come up. Move freely on it.

Lesson Plan Fifty-One

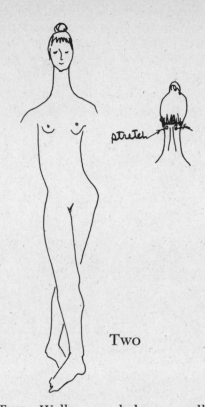

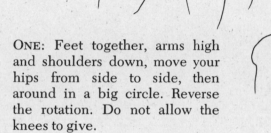

TWO

ONE: Feet together, arms high and shoulders down, move your hips from side to side, then around in a big circle. Reverse the rotation. Do not allow the knees to give.

ONE

TWO: Walk on a balance, well tucked-in and with hips moving in a small, constrained circle. Stretch from the spaces at the base of the head in the back. As one hip is out to the side, the opposite leg should move forward.

THREE: Up on toes with legs apart, pull up out of hips and press back against the knees. Bring the torso forward from the hips. Stay on toes, let the knees give and spread wide as your arms swing back and your waist sinks toward the floor. The chest, head and buttocks stay up higher than the waist. Your arms move back, then up as you tuck in, pushing forward at the knees, then at the crotch, and come up into a full stretch. Repeat.

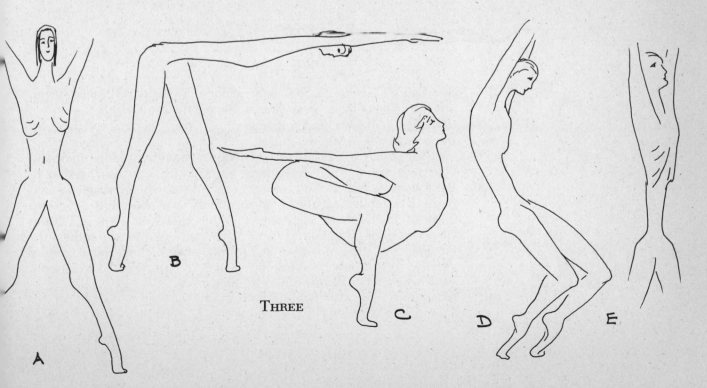

A B THREE C D E

FOUR: Sit cross-legged. Try to get the knees to lie flat on the floor. Cross your arms with the hands resting on opposite thighs. Bend back at the waist, trying to get the top of your head on the floor. Do this slowly. Raise at Center. If necessary, use hands and arms to help you.

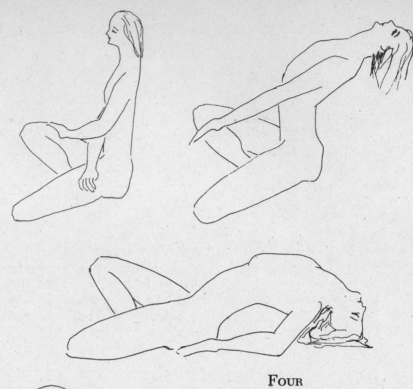

FIVE: While seated, stretch up tall through your head. Turn the head to one side, stretch up through the chin and slowly turn your head to the other side. Roll your head around to the back, to the side and to the front and then to the other side. Reverse the direction. The entire exercise is done very slowly.

FOUR

SIX

SIX: Lying flat on your back with arms at sides, raise your chest until the top of your head touches the floor. Relax down, tucking in, and bring your knees up so that your feet are flat on the floor. Raise your pelvis from the floor, pushing the crotch up high, come down and straighten your legs. Come up through the chest Center into a sitting position and slowly come down, rounding your back and feeling each vertebra until you are flat on the floor. The head is the last down. Repeat the sequence.

SEVEN: Stand with legs apart and swing both arms up together to one side, down, up, down, up and around over head and down, up to the other side. Repeat. Let the knees give as you swing the arms down. On the overhead swing, make a half-turn. Move freely on it.

Lesson Plan Fifty-Two

ONE: Start with the Jacob's Ladder stretch.

TWO: Stretch through the arms, which are extended out to the sides at shoulder height. Stretch out as far as possible through one arm and shoulder, then the other. Repeat. Then, keeping arms extended, stretch to both sides at the same time and roll or turn shoulders forward and backward. Slowly roll the head around following the movement of the shoulders. Reverse. Repeat.

Two

THREE

THREE: Stand with one foot in front of the other. The arm on the side of the back foot stretches up as high as possible, while the arm on the side of the forward foot pulls strongly forward at shoulder height. Walk two, three. On the third step, the "up" arm comes down forward as the other arm moves up to meet it. Then squeeze your extended arms together and bend from your waist, head leading, to the side of the back leg. Cross the front leg around and pivot. Repeat to the other side. Repeat.

FOUR: Stand with feet together and bend to the side at your waist with the head leading. Slowly raise and lower the leg on the opposite side. Move the leg up as high as possible. Do it alternating sides.

FIVE: Stand with feet together. Swing one leg out to the side and hop to that side with the other foot. The free leg then swings across to the other side and the standing leg hops back that way. Swing out again and jump in the direction of the swing, landing on the swinging leg with foot down flat and knee bent. Repeat, alternating legs.

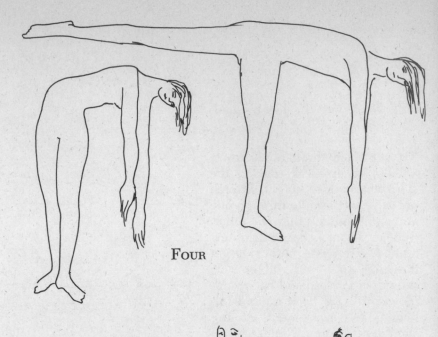

FOUR

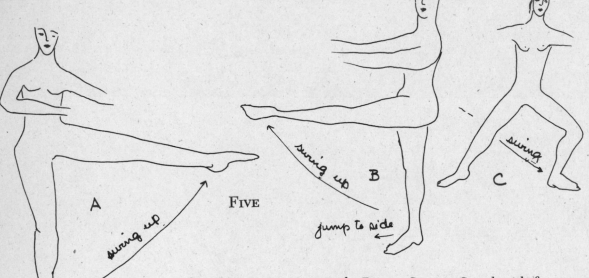

A

swing up

jump to side

FIVE

swing up B

jump to side

swing C

SIX: Lie on your stomach. Bring one heel up toward the buttocks, then bring your leg up off the floor, keeping the knee bent. The hipbone stays down on the floor. Come down slowly and repeat, alternating legs.

SEVEN: Stand with feet together. Step to one side. The other foot steps across in front and the back leg steps out to its side. The other leg now swings up across as the standing leg jumps. The swinging leg swings back to its own side; step and repeat from side to side. Repeat.

EIGHT: Exercise Nine in Lesson Forty-Eight.

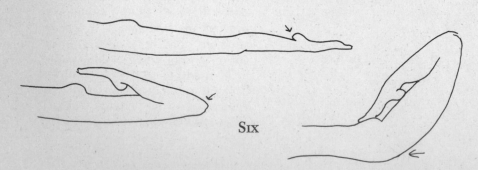

SIX

Lesson Plan Fifty-Three

ONE: Stand with legs apart and arms stretched up apart over your head. Join your hands behind your head. Lift one side, stretching at the underarm. Lead with the elbow of the lower arm and make a tremendous twist to the back, pressing down with the leading shoulder. Reverse, repeat.

ONE

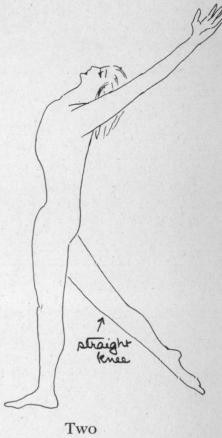

TWO: Stand with feet together and exhale, head and arms hanging forward from the Center. Inhale, raising the arms and head and lifting one leg somewhat to the back. As you exhale, the head, arms and leg drop, further each time, and then lift higher each time on the inhalation. Change legs after each series of breathings.

TWO

THREE: Stand with your head down and arms extended to the front. Inhale, and the head moves to the back from the Center. The arms come straight up and one leg moves up to the back. Exhale, and the arms come forward, the head drops and the back leg comes down. Repeat, changing legs. Move to the back by putting your weight on the back foot and bringing the front leg up to the back.

THREE

FOUR: The dance of mourning is done on the breath, using opposite arm and leg. Beat the breast with clenched fists, first one fist, then the other. The head leads in a forward and backward motion. Move freely on it, in a frenzy of mourning, allowing your feelings to dictate.

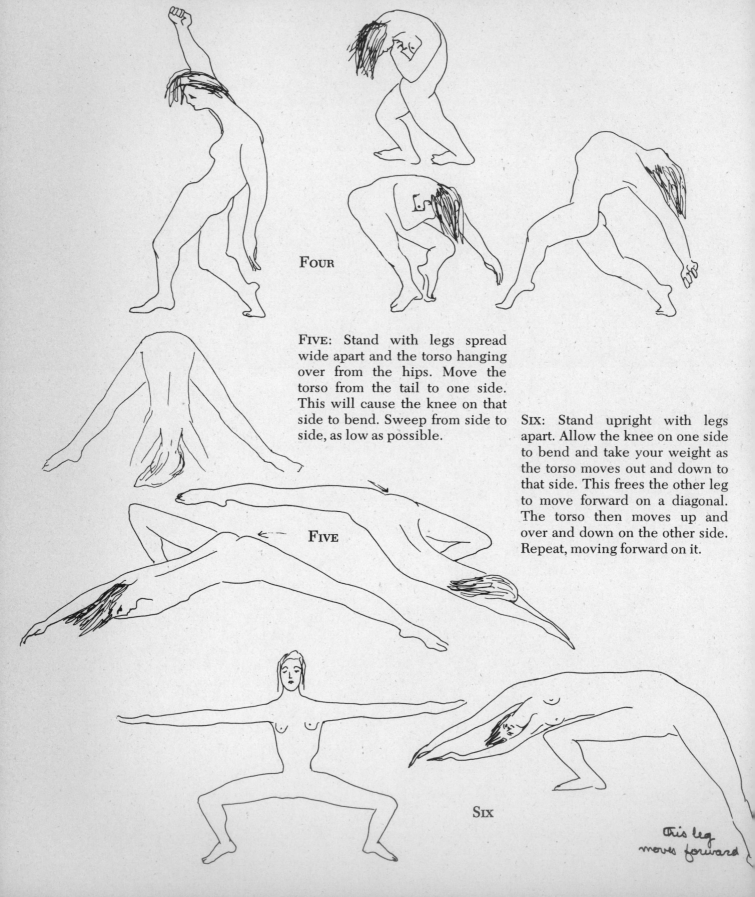

FOUR

FIVE: Stand with legs spread wide apart and the torso hanging over from the hips. Move the torso from the tail to one side. This will cause the knee on that side to bend. Sweep from side to side, as low as possible.

SIX: Stand upright with legs apart. Allow the knee on one side to bend and take your weight as the torso moves out and down to that side. This frees the other leg to move forward on a diagonal. The torso then moves up and over and down on the other side. Repeat, moving forward on it.

FIVE

SIX

this leg
moves forward

SEVEN: Stand with legs apart and arms pulled up. Push your pelvis around in a circle against thigh resistance, i.e., the knees and thighs work in the opposite direction to the pelvis. Repeat circling the other way.

EIGHT: Stand with legs apart and swing arms from side to side, down around and up over your head. Leap-turn as the arms swing up and over. Repeat to the other side. Repeat.

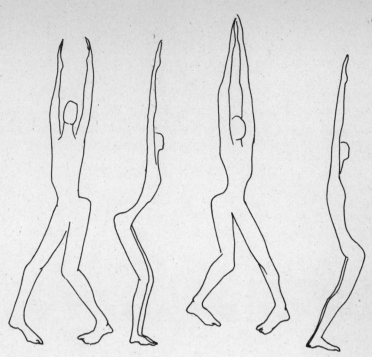

SEVEN

6
On Teaching

Teaching is the experience of the moment. Go into yourself to draw this experience out. You do not want to show how well you can do a thing, you want to awaken the inner sense of movement in your pupils, and to get rid of their self-consciousness. Assume that you and they know nothing so that each time it will be a new experience, a new creation.

Pupils reflect the truth that is in a teacher. The best and truest way to teach is to practice so that you yourself unfold, for until you do you can't help others much. Use your own intuition and experience in working out your teaching, and the result will take care of itself.

Prepare fresh lessons every day, drawing from the wellsprings of being. The spoken word is creative. The imagination connected with the intellect is creative. Imagination without intellect leads only to fantasizing, while the intellect without imagination is sterile.

The parts of the body become free through the use of images. Movement on command is just exercise, without joy. But pure joy and spontaneity open the way to unfolding, and joy is more important than correctness of execution. Do not expect students to do a movement correctly the first time; concentrate instead on the quality of rhythm that they get unconsciously through the symbols. Everything takes work and application. Your concern is with what is happening now, not with the future result. Do not be caught by the outward aspect. Let the movement unfold and know that the same universal cause constantly operates and new effects always happen.

A beginners' class is a breaking-up process, breaking up rigidities of body and mind. The mind is restless and needs variety. Give rhythms that stress emotional *and* physical release. Work on the *down* and you will get the reflex *up*.

Think of your pupils as individuals and give the kinds of symbols they will respond to. People have different awareness, but all have possibilities. If they do not get the quality of the symbol, don't stop them and tell them they are wrong. Don't talk over their heads. Keep quietly returning to the symbol as simply as possible. Don't hinder. Feel the symbol yourself. Move with them, not for them. Guide them and leave them alone. Expression comes from the SELF, and its form is different in everyone. If pupils begin to imitate, stop them and change the symbol, no matter how well they imitate. We do not want copies. We want the natural individual flow of rhythm.

Teach differently to different ages. Watch pupils as they come in. Do not acknowledge their moods. If they come in upset, see to it they leave happy and unfolded.

Tense, brittle pupils need to let go completely before rhythm can flow. As a teacher, you must learn to look deeper than the surface. There are some people who are so tense that they cannot respond to imaginative symbols. Give these people directions to hold in mind until the continuity becomes established. Then emphasize smoothness and flow. For tense people, stress feeling. Give them work to soften and heat them, without the responsibility of following precise directions.

Soft people need a lot of resistive work so that their movement will not be too easy. Stress coordination. Have them move from intense inner feeling and with much pressure.

The lesson plans are adaptable for children's work. Identify in your mind with children, and you will know which lessons to use and how to adapt them. Let music play a dominant part.

You have to put yourself in the place of a child or adolescent in order to teach him sympathetically and creatively. Give symbols to stimulate imagination. He then gets inside of what he is doing, and this will carry over to other lessons.

Children are growing. See that they are kept stretched open with plenty of space between the units (see page 19) of the body. In general, keep them stretching up by leaping, reaching. Give bursting movements, such as firecrackers shooting out. Give elephant movements on, on and around, following the swing of the arms. You can give them the sense of sweeping, cutting, clearing, as if the arms were a scythe, or have them stretch as if they were sweeping the sky with a broom.

All children should have the whole cycle of work. Stress balance on a straight line, standing tall, whether on toes or not. Coordinate the movements of opposite arms and legs, especially when arms have to be kept shoulder-high. Teach dance through form, but do not let it become formal or stilted.

If children are very nervous and high-strung, relax them with big leaps. Let them imagine dawn, with the sun leaping from mountaintop to mountaintop, or a walk in the early morning in the country. The walk leads logically into a run, the run into a leap, and slows back down into a walk.

When they are tired, have them do shoulder movements and then gradually slow down, thinking of energy leaking away to the earth and being absorbed by the earth. Then soft, restful floorwork and up into something fey and lyrical—wind through pinetrees, a waltz or something with a soft underswing. Circles are always soothing.

If some spontaneous action comes from a student, make use of it. Children have such a keen dramatic sense that it is wise to give only the initial movement with the feeling or quality you want, such as lightness, airiness, roundness in tumbling. You should be constantly expanding their areas of consciousness through the kinesthetic sense, as applied to music and dramatic material. Freedom and balance come through the combination of directed activity and the expansion of consciousness. For example, have them imagine that they are horses stamping on a summer night to get rid of flies bothering them. This will strengthen the reflexes of the ankles, knees and hips. Or you might talk of sprites or elves in the woods—anything that appeals to and enriches the imagination. Children will take these things and render them back to you a hundredfold, in exquisite drama, talking, giggling, hide-and-seek, imaginative revelations. You see moving, liquid music. Direct the dance along the channels they choose and see that it completes itself. That is a cycle, a wholeness. Give them credit by praising and become a part of the drama they are unfolding. For example, they will usually begin to whoop as soon as you say "Indian." But you can say, "I see the Indians sneaking up to the bears. They are crouching, walking in the tall grasses and *they do not use the war whoop until* the animal is captured. Then they WAR WHOOP as they crouch over, making a heel-toe movement, so. That is their victory dance." Enter into the story with them and the corrections will cease to be corrections to them. You will be one of them, which is as it should be. Do not single out any one pupil for corrections. Give correction meant for one to the class in general. Too much free movement can become chaotic. There must be freedom in law. You know that the teaching is coming along when there is more and more order in free movement.

You will often see a pupil doing something during one movement which will give you an idea for the next. You will also find your own body telling you what to do. Rhythm releases creativity, and the teacher must be aware, thinking creatively throughout each lesson. Yet no matter how you use the lesson plans, whether you follow them or use them as a jumping-off point, there are certain principles that should be adhered to.

Begin every lesson with a complete stretch. If you give a symbol or a reason for the stretch it will come alive. Some work should be given on the Center, the spine, the lower back, or the tuck-in and the up-through. During the lesson, try to give two periods of creative work and one of rest, or movement in rest. To move in rest means to continue doing the movement, but in a completely relaxed, almost imperceptible fashion. Give soft stretches during the spring and summer.

Give energetic shreds, leaps and the like in winter and autumn.

A good lesson plan for beginners contains 1) stretch, 2) work on feeling the Center or head, arms and legs operating from Center, 3) chaotic free movement, 4) animal rhythms, 5) resting and stretching on the floor; work with a symbol, 6) free movement in form.

Remember the importance of the beginning stretch. It makes for long lines. Spinal stretching makes spaces between the vertebrae so that they do not settle down on one another. The stretch gives space for a complete tuck-in and for free movement.

Rhythm begins in the mind, then the body moves in rhythm. Never force the body. Seduce it into movement and allow it to come along in its own way. You can often get the spine to loosen more easily if you give movements with the feet apart. Give heavy downward pressures for the feet. This causes the nerves to waken and will lead to a rebound up. Liken the spine to a hollow stem with sap flowing through it. This makes the spine feel open and alive. Think of it as growing rather than stretching. For work on the straight line, do not think of yourself standing straight: think of a straight line moving from under the earth to the heavens. Rest on the straight line, it will strengthen inner balance.

Last thoughts: Everything must be allowed to leak away. Then you experience cause, operation and effect. Trust this cause. It is love. The operation is joy, and the effect is beauty.

The purpose of teaching is to unfold the individual to his capacity. You will know when your work comes to fruition. The higher mind will function through the body. Light and spirit radiate through matter—the person looks radiant and his skin changes color. Joy is there to be seen. Joy is the opening of the inspirational vein.

There are two aspects to a dance lesson, technique and art. Technique is the basis of how you use your instrument, the body. Art is creativity, that which flows through and uses the instrument for its own purposes.

THINK about this. DO IT. LOVE IT. TEACH IT. DREAM IT.